The Intentional MINISTER

4 *Powerful Steps to Determining, Implementing, and Fulfilling Your Ministry Priorities*

THOMAS GOODMAN

BROADMAN
&HOLMAN
PUBLISHERS

Nashville, Tennessee

4230-15
0-8054-3015-6

Dewey Decimal Classification: 253
Subject Heading: PASTORAL WORK
Library of Congress Card Catalog Number: 94-9692
Printed in the United States of America

Unless otherwise noted, Scripture quotations are from the Holy Bible, *New International Version,* copyright © 1973, 1978, 1984 by International Bible Society. Scriptures marked (NEB) are from *The New English Bible,* copyright © The Delegates of the Oxford University Press and the Syndics of the Cambridge University Press, 1961, 1970, reprinted by permission; (RSV) the *Revised Standard Version of the Bible,* copyrighted 1946, 1952, © 1971, 1973; (AMP) *The Amplified Bible,* Old Testament, copyright © 1962, 1964 by Zondervan Publishing House, used by permission; and (KJV) the *King James Version.*

Library of Congress Cataloging-in-Publication Data
Goodman, Thomas, 1961–
    The intentional minister: 4 powerful steps to determining, implementing, and fulfilling your ministry priorities / Thomas Goodman.
        p. cm.
    ISBN 0-8054-3015-6
    1. Clergy—Office. 2. Pastoral theology. I Title.
    BV660.2.G57   1994   94-9692
    253'.2—dc20   CIP

CONTENTS

Introduction / 1

1. Where There Is No Vision, the Minister Perishes! / 7

2. The First Step: Create Your "Ministry Manifesto" / 25

3. The Second Step: A Personal Checkup / 55

4. The Third Step: Set Goals for Personal Improvement / 75

5. The Fourth Step: Set Action Plans / 93

6. Now What? / 115

Notes / 133

INTRODUCTION

"He Died Climbing"

> — A monument reportedly raised in the Alps in
> honor of a faithful guide who perished while as-
> cending a peak to rescue a stranded tourist.

GARY ALLEN KNOWS ABOUT unfinished business. In 1979, the church he pastored in Illinois sold their building, bought property, and began construction on a new structure. No one was worried about securing financing since interest rates were low. Building costs were rising, though, and so the decision was made to sell the old property and start building on the new property right away.

Then it happened. Before the church could get a bank to commit money to complete the project it had already started, interest rates suddenly skyrocketed. Rates rose from 8 percent to between 17 and 23 percent. Suddenly, the church was stuck with an unfinished building and no way to finance its completion. During the two years spent looking for financing, the cement shell of the building became a home for pigeons. Allen says that every day he would walk through the empty shell of that building and cry and pray. In frustration he would throw pebbles at the birds to shoo them away from his unfinished project.[1]

The apostle Paul regarded his life as an unfinished project. He said, "Forgetting what is behind and straining toward what is ahead, I press on toward the goal to win the prize for which God has called me heavenward in Christ Jesus." [2] That our lives are incomplete ought to evoke more than a shrug of the shoulders. We ought to be like that converted rabbi who pressed on toward the goal. We ought to be like that Illinois pastor who daily walked through the wind-swept shell of his building, crying over its incompletion and praying for its completion.

In other words, we ought to have inspirational dissatisfaction. That is what John Haggai calls it. It is a restlessness of heart that comes from recognizing the distance between where you are and where you want to be. Without it we make truce with the status quo and quit struggling against our shortcomings. With it we have the motivation to make the changes necessary to be all God wants us to be.

I THINK I'VE FOUND YOU!

Assuming you do have an inspirational dissatisfaction toward your ministry, how can you make your frustration constructive? The best way to turn dissatisfaction into positive action is to define where you want to be and then set measurable goals to get there.

This book is designed to help you do just that.

Most of us have read books or attended seminars on planning and goal-setting for the programs we lead. If you have experienced the positive changes that come from leading your church to set and pursue goals under a well-defined mission statement, then you know the benefits of the process. But have you ever *applied that process to your own growth as a minister?*

Vance Havner reportedly said, "The devil will let a preacher prepare a sermon if it will keep him from preparing himself." Perhaps some of us must confess that the devil has let us have our well-developed ministries only because all the work has kept us from becoming well-developed ministers. We certainly need material that will help us evaluate and improve the programs we lead. But we also need a "how-to" manual for personal evaluation and goal-setting.

I can imagine some readers have already put the book down at this point. "A mission statement? Too dry," one will say. "Goals? Too managerial," another will say. "Action plans? They will stifle the free flow of the Spirit in my ministry," a third will say.

Believe me, if I could I would avoid words from management textbooks like "action plans" and "objectives." But the words merely label the steps of a process we must all take—consciously or unconsciously—if we want to improve. When a self-improvement plan is understood in this way, reliance upon the Spirit is heightened, not minimized. The work of the Spirit does not make it unnecessary to plan for improvement. The Spirit makes it *possible!*

The apostle Paul is an example of a church leader whose stated mission intensified his dependence upon the Spirit. We see this combination of being *purpose-driven* and *Spirit-empowered* most clearly in Colossians 1:28–29. In fact, I consider the following text a scriptural justification for my book:

> We proclaim him, admonishing and teaching everyone with all wisdom, so that we may present everyone perfect in Christ. *To this end* I labor, struggling with all *his energy*, which so powerfully works in me [emphasis added].

Did you notice that Paul did not hesitate to join in the same sentence both the objective of his labors and the power of the Spirit? The minister who has an inspirational dissatisfaction with his or her work will find that setting the objectives of his labors actually intensifies reliance on the Holy Spirit, just as it did for the apostle Paul. We need the wisdom the Spirit provides to define our mission, and we need the power the Spirit provides to fulfill our mission.

This book was born out of inspirational dissatisfaction, and my prayer is that it will be used by other church leaders who have such a mood toward their own ministries. Let me suggest some ways you can put this book to good use.

- Work through the material on your own. Since each chapter builds on the previous ones, be sure to complete the activities at the end of each chapter. Your time in this book will be more productive if you will do so.

- Even better, introduce this book to a prayer partner or a support group. Review the chapters together and report your completed activities to each other. Accountability will make the activities in this book more effective.

- If you lead a staff through annual planning, spend some time going through the four steps outlined in this book. While church programs need review and improvement, so do those who *lead* the programs. In fact, the time given to staff for self-renewal has a direct impact on the quality of church programs. Put a copy of *The Intentional Minister* in the hands of each minister at your church.

I hope you will find this book to be both *informational* and *inspirational.* I've read too many books that are long on one characteristic only to be short on the other. To fulfill the aim of making this an informative book, I have broken down the self-improvement process into four steps; and I have explained each step in detail using the professional expertise of consultants and the personal experience of ministers. To fulfill the aim of making an inspiring book, I have provided challenges and suggestions that should stir you to begin your own process of self-improvement.

You will also find references to a number of resources that will help you improve as a minister. In addition, I have illustrated the material with objectives and goals that ministers in various positions could have set. All the examples are fictitious, but I am indebted to the experiences shared by friends and associates who serve as pastors and staff members. My hope is that the men and women who serve as ministers will be able to identify with the fictional scenarios.

By the way, you will notice that throughout the book I refer to members of the pastor's staff with either the pronoun "he" or "she," while I refer to pastors with the pronoun "he." No doubt some will be disappointed that I have not illustrated my material with references to women in the pastorate, while some will be dismayed that I make references to women on staff at all. However, the book was not written to defend a particular viewpoint toward women in church leadership, and I hope that my illustrations will not be distracting.

My aim is to help ministers convert their inspirational dissatisfaction into a plan for self-improvement. I like the way John Haggai qualifies the mood—inspirational dissatisfaction. It is not a paralyzing self-pity over one's shortcomings. Instead, it is a restlessness that inspires one to improve. In *Lead On!* Haggai wrote:

> Inspirational dissatisfaction is different from a morose, brooding, cynical dissatisfaction that impels one to withdraw into a shell or, on the other hand, aggressively criticize the alleged reasons for his dissatisfaction. Inspirational dissatisfaction inspires a person to high attainment.[3]

The same sun that hardens the clay melts the wax, goes the saying. For one, the realization that he is not the minister he wants to be sends him into either hopeless dejection or vigorous self-justification. For another, the same realization energizes him to improve in the power of the Spirit. This book was written for the second kind of minister—I think I've found you.

MANY THANKS

"What do you have that you did not receive?" Paul asked the prideful Corinthians.[4]

I am grateful for what I received in the process of writing this book. I am grateful for receiving the gift of time from two churches. I researched and wrote this book while serving two wonderful churches—Riverdale Baptist Church in Baton Rouge, Louisiana, and the First Baptist Church of Eastland, Texas. Also, I am grateful for receiving the clerical help of two fine secretaries at those churches—Angela Vanveckhoven in Baton Rouge and Joanna Maynard in Eastland.

I am grateful for the suggestions of numerous associates in the ministry. My special thanks to seven pastors in Baton Rouge, Louisiana, to Rick Grant and Ricky Guenther of my own staff, and to Dr. Damon Shook and his staff at Champion Forest Baptist Church in Houston, Texas. These persons allowed me to present this material to them in a seminar format, and their review of the material was helpful. Also, my thanks go to Jack Ridlehoover who reviewed the manuscript before I submitted it to Broadman & Holman Publishers. Jack now serves other ministers as president of Minister's Mentoring and Counseling Service in Abilene, Texas. Jack offered many encouraging comments.

Finally, I am grateful for receiving the support and unconditional love of my wife, Diane; my two sons, Michael and Stephen; and my parents, Charles and Ellen Goodman. I love you all.

WHERE THERE IS NO VISION, THE MINISTER PERISHES!

For most of us, it is easier to think about how to get what we want than to know what exactly we should want.

— Robert Bellah
Habits of the Heart

M Y LITTLE SONS HAVE A SAYING when I walk into their playroom and find a drink spilled or a toy broken. "It was just an accident," they say. "I didn't do it on purpose." They have found that I will not scold them for something that was not done "on purpose." Regarding the ministries to which Christ has called us grown-ups, though, we are scolded precisely for the things that are not done on purpose. Jesus expects us to invest ourselves in the work of His kingdom deliberately—intentionally—with the aim of hearing His assessment, "Well done."[1]

Think about a minister who has impressed you. Why do you admire that person? In the last month, have you consciously done anything to develop those same qualities in yourself? Now, think about a minister that you do not respect. What is it about that person that has disappointed you? Have you been doing anything to ensure that you do not walk down the same road he has taken? We need to express our idea of a well-done ministry, and we need a plan for achieving that vision. We need to be intentional ministers!

LEARNING FROM EXPERIENCE

Where there is no vision, the minister perishes. Really, the wise man said that without a vision the people perish,[2] but I discovered both statements to be worthy warnings. When one congregation I served was without a sense of purpose, we were vulnerable to self-doubt, squandered resources, and hostile division. Without a *personal* vision, I ran the risk of "perishing," too. Providentially, I found out that the same process that restored a sense of purpose in our church was helpful for restoring my vision, also.

Let me explain. Several years ago a church I served was in aching need of a defined purpose. The congregation was split in half regarding the renovation of our facilities. Half of us felt that the twenty-year-old worship center was too worn to attract the affluent families that had moved in around the church. The other half was not convinced the renovation was needed. Over time, it dawned on me that the people actually disagreed on something more fundamental than new carpeting. The renovation issue simply brought to the surface the competing agendas within our congregation. The people were without a vision; they were in danger of "perishing" as a congregation. They needed to arrive at an agreement over the purpose of our church's existence.

I led the church through a four-step process of long-range planning. First, we studied the Scriptures in which the ideal of the church is described. From this study we prepared a written statement of our objectives. This statement became the expression of our vision—our ideal for the church. Second, we used the objectives to examine our ministry and determine improvements that we would make together. Third, we established long-range goals. Then, fourth, we set a plan of action to achieve each goal.

As we wrote our statement of objectives and used it for evaluation and planning, I noticed that the process began to transform our church. I was certainly pleased with the fresh life, renewed commitment, and increased numbers. But even as the church was enjoying renewal, I was sending out resumés. The failure to lead the congregation to renovate had left me with self-doubts, resentment, and an oppressive weariness. Then, during a morning devotional it hit me: What had transformed the church could work for me, too. I decided to write a statement of my objectives as a pastor—a "ministry manifesto," so to speak—and use it for my own personal evaluation and planning. I decided to become an intentional minister.

WHY YOU NEED A MINISTRY MANIFESTO

While others refer to it as a statement of objectives or a personal mission statement, I have always preferred the word *manifesto*. A *manifesto* is a public declaration of intent. Even the words sound robust and stirring—"ministry manifesto." With a ministry manifesto, I imagine myself decisively pounding my fist in my palm and declaring my intent to fulfill my call to the ministry. My ministry manifesto is my defiant shout into the faces of those who oppose my ministry: the world, the devil, and my own flesh.

Why do we need to evaluate and plan our work against a written statement of personal objectives? Through my experience, I've found several urgent reasons for a minister to take the time and trouble to prepare a written declaration of his ideals. As you read the following paragraphs, make a mental checkmark next to the reason that best persuades you to write a ministry manifesto.

A Framework for Ministry

By defining our concept of the ideal ministry, we have a comprehensive overview of ministry by which all the parts can be seen. Church members will often call me simply, "The Preacher." Of course, I am not simply a preacher. I am not purely a counselor, a program leader, or an administrator, either. I am all of these—and more! Designing a statement of objectives enables us to appreciate the whole picture of ministry in which the parts are set.

Ministers who have not defined the scope of their work may perfect one segment of the ministry only to have the lingering suspicion that they have neglected some other unidentified part of the calling. Ministers who have not constructed a comprehensive model for their work may address whatever task demands the most attention instead of striving for balance. Ministers who have not determined what their divine assignment entails find themselves attending seminars or buying books based on what catches their attention instead of on what will help them develop some aspect of their work.

A Prevention Against Burnout

A newspaper misprinted the weather forecast in the morning edition, leaving out the word "rain." The forecast read, "There is only a twenty percent chance of tomorrow." Have you ever felt as if that was not a misprint? Ministers know that burnout is one of our professional risks.

What a vivid word! *Burnout.* When a fire burns out, what does it leave behind? Gray ashes, darkness, coldness. When zeal fizzles out, what does it leave behind? Gray purposelessness, dark hopelessness, cold cynicism. Even our "humor" becomes sarcastic and biting! Ministers suffer burnout either because of internal or external factors.

First, consider the internal factor that leads to burnout: Some ministers confess that they do not have satisfaction in their work. No matter how much they do, they never know when they have done enough. No matter how well they perform, they never know when they have done their work well enough. Eventually they begin showing the symptoms of burnout—cynicism, weariness, irritability, and self-pity.

Then there is the external factor that leads to burnout: Some of us serve churches where dreams go to die. We can keenly identify with Jeremiah when he said, "Oh, that I had in the desert a lodging place for travelers,/ so that I might leave my people and go away from them;/ for they are all . . . a crowd of unfaithful people."[3] As a result, a bitter anger or an apathetic hopelessness descends over our weekly routine.

A combination of both external and internal factors sent me into sulking depression several years ago. Thank God, the process of preparing my ministry manifesto helped me to rise, phoenix-like, out of the ashes of burnout. By referring frequently to my manifesto over the years, I have managed to stay out of that dreadful state.

I am told that in the days of stone gristmills, the millers had to be careful to keep grain between the grinding millstones always. Otherwise, the massive stones would grind each other to bits. The gristmill had to be engaged in its purpose or it would self-destruct. What is true in the mill is true in the ministry. If we are not engaged in an intentional ministry, all of our labor will simply grind us to bits. In his classic little pamphlet, *The Tyranny of the Urgent*, Charles Hummel wrote, "The only alternative to frustration [Hummel's word for burnout?] is to be sure that we are doing what God wants. Nothing substitutes for knowing that this day, this hour, in this place we are doing the will of the Father."[4]

Better Stewardship

One consultant identified what he called the "top fifteen time-wasters worldwide." He based the list on a sampling of managers in fourteen countries. Number five on the list was "lack of objectives, priorities, and deadlines."[5]

With a statement of objectives we will be better stewards of the time, talents, and energies that God has given us.

In New Testament times, a steward was to manage his master's property according to his master's wishes. The concept was so familiar that it became a key image in the teachings of Jesus, Paul, and Peter regarding the Christian mission.[6] By preparing a statement of objectives, we will define how our Master wishes us to manage the time, talent, and energy He has loaned to us.

How often we ministers give ourselves to the "good" projects at the expense of the "best" projects! This is especially true among "people persons" who are eager to honor any request made of them. Reviewing my weekly schedule against my manifesto helps me to set boundaries and say "no" to certain requests. In addition, it helps me monitor the amount of time and energy I am giving to certain activities.

Motivating Power

Knowing that God has called us into the ministry—and knowing what tasks that call implies—has kept more than one minister going when the circumstances were difficult. No person can survive the ministry who does not sense that calling. When finances are thin, when human opposition attacks his vision, when he's surrounded by more silly people than spiritual people, he must be able to reach back into his own history with God and say, "But I was *called* to this!"

At other times the problem is not what is around him but what is in him. Immorality tempts him; he begins to sense a laziness about his labors; he takes on a cynical edge that nearly despairs of ever seeing fruit from his work; inner fears of inadequacy nearly paralyze him. In these times he needs to be able to say, "I will be held accountable for how I followed God's call!"

There is a motivating power in putting into a written statement *that* God has called you and *what* God has called you to do. Ari Kiev wrote:

> Without a central [objective], your thoughts become worrisome; your confidence and morale may be undermined, and you may be led to the feared circumstances. Without [an objective], you will focus on your weaknesses, and the possibilities of errors and criticism. This will foster indecision, procrastination, and inadequacy and will impede the development of your potential.[7]

Consultants in the field of management and researchers in the field of psychology have confirmed the importance of goal-setting for motivation. When we define our ministerial objectives, our jobs take on an energizing urgency. George Sweazey addressed this issue to Princeton seminary students years ago. He said that without a time clock or a supervisor, ministers must drive themselves. Sweazy observed:

> The hardest part of his job is the endless strain it puts upon the will. He has to fight unusual excuses for slacking off. . . . The minister needs urgencies that will sting him wide awake on the morning after an evening meeting. He needs vivid incentives that will propel him into the heaviest tasks with a lean, hard-driving, tenacious eagerness.[8]

A manifesto gives a minister incentives that are vivid enough and urgent enough to motivate.

Meaningful Productivity

Working under a manifesto will help you become an accomplishmentist! The famous management consultant, Peter Drucker, points out that the English language has a word for *activist*, meaning "one who is active." But there is no word for *accomplishmentist*, meaning "one who accomplishes something." He wonders, wryly, if the Western world does not have the word because so few could be characterized by the word.[9]

If we desire to produce more in areas that we know are important, we need a statement of objectives. The key phrase is "in areas we know are important." There is a vast difference between being busy and being effective! Doug Sherman, a Christian career consultant, remembered a pilot he trained during his days as an Air Force fighter trainer. During an extended flight, the trainee began to drift off course. Sherman asked him if he knew where he was going. He replied, "No, sir—but we're sure making good time!"[10] Ministers, too, can become caught up in the breathtaking pace of their projects and lose sight of the reason for the work. We can get so enmeshed in the activity that we lose sight of why we are doing it, and the activity itself becomes a false goal. Ministry descends into minutia when church leaders work without a clear idea of what well-done service looks like.

How can we escape? Each time we consider investing ourselves in an activity, we need to ask, "Is this in keeping with what God has called me to be and do? Would another activity do more to help move me toward those objectives?"

A Renewed Sense of the Dignity of Our Calling

Have you made a mental check mark yet next to any of the first five reasons to prepare a ministry manifesto? How about this sixth reason? By clarifying our vocational objectives, we enrich our concept of the ministerial task. Paul told his young friend at Ephesus that pastoring was a "noble task"[11]; however, we live in an age when the work of a minister is denigrated. In such an age, we must regain the dignity of our calling.

In his Yale lectures during the opening years of this century, John Henry Jowett discussed the importance of operating under a "glorious and wonderful" image of the ministry. His advice is still timely in the closing years of this century:

> Emerson has somewhere said that men whose duties are done beneath lofty and stately domes acquire a dignified stride and a certain stateliness of demeanour. And preachers of the gospel,

whose work is done beneath the lofty dome of some glorious and wonderful conception of their ministry, will acquire a certain largeness of demeanour in which flippancy and trivialities cannot breathe. *"I shall run the way of Thy commandments when Thou shalt enlarge my heart."*[12]

An Outline to Explain Our Priorities to Others

A ministry manifesto gives us a tool to explain our work to others in concise terms. In his book about role conflicts in the ministry, Donald Smith points out:

> If one is to minimize ambiguity in the expectations of others, he must also minimize it in himself. . . . The person who is not clear as to who he is, what he believes, what his understanding of the church and ministry is, what his goals are, and where his strengths and weaknesses lie, is not well prepared to evaluate or relate to the expectations of others for his performance.[13]

With clearly defined objectives we are able to explain our priorities to formal evaluators, self-appointed critics, and search committees from other churches.

First, a written manifesto will help clear up the occasional but inevitable misunderstandings with personnel committees and boards. Conversations regarding the perceived inadequacies in a minister's performance often generate more emotional heat than rational light. The minister who can present his or her priorities to the evaluators will provide a helpful framework for formal evaluations.

In addition, by having a clear concept of what we have been called to do, we can better handle our self-appointed critics. In a popular witnessing tract, one of the statements says that God loves you and has a wonderful plan for your life. Many of us have found that certain people have a "wonderful plan" for our lives, too! When others try to set our agenda, we must be able to explain our objectives to them. We are able to do that only after we have settled the issue of what Christ has called us to be and do.

Also, when prospective churches interview you, you will be ready to share what they can expect of you. Your priorities, your strengths and weaknesses, and your work schedule can all be discussed in the framework of what you believe God has called you to be and do.

Freedom from the Popularity Polls

"Hello," said the cheery voice answering the telephone, "Church of God Grill." When Charles Paul Conn ran across this unusual name in the "Restaurant" section of the Yellow Pages, the name aroused his curiosity. Conn dialed the restaurant number and the manager answered the phone. Conn asked how his restaurant had been given such a peculiar name. The man replied, "Well, we had a little mission down here, and we started selling chicken dinners after church on Sunday to help pay the bills. People liked the chicken, and we did such a good business, that eventually we cut back on the church service. After a while we just closed down the church altogether and kept on serving the chicken dinners. We kept the name we started with, and that's Church of God Grill."[14]

The leaders of this enterprise in Altanta had no strong sense of purpose, so they drifted toward the activities that had the most positive public response. Likewise, if we ministers have not defined what Christ has called us to be and do, then we will be subject to whatever role or activity elicits a positive reaction from the crowds. Determining our concept of ideal ministry will deliver us from bondage to applause.

Certainly, our ministries ought to be "popular," in the sense that our preaching and programs must connect with the hearts and minds of the people we serve. We ought to care how our work is perceived by the very persons our work is meant to benefit. Still, the work of our ministries must not be limited to what actions or events result in the greatest vocal approval.

Mothers do not prepare meals simply by what their children demand. Coaches do not order drills simply by what their athletes enjoy. By doing ministry under a clear concept of our calling, we will give people what they need, not simply what they want.

Setting the Example

When our staff and volunteer leaders see us establishing priorities and setting goals, they will be more likely to do so. John Alexander addresses leaders of any organization, not just churches, when he insists:

> Every leader should have two sets of objectives, goals and standards: one for himself as a person and one for the team which he leads. . . . Within an organization, construction of annual and long-range plans should begin at the top. Let the chief executive first construct his own goals and standards and circulate copies throughout the movement. . . . A person is more likely to participate [in goal-setting] if he sees his supervisor working according to goals and standards.[15]

It would thrill most ministers to see Sunday School teachers pursuing personal goals to increase class enrollment or deacons achieving self-made goals to increase their in-home visits. If we want this to happen within our churches, we must be willing to set the example.

A Working Definition of Success

What tasks must we perform to hear Jesus say, "Well done, good and faithful servant"? That is the question we are answering when we write ministry manifestos.

In their book, *Liberating Ministry from the Success Syndrome*, Kent and Barbara Hughes recounted the crisis that led to their decision to clarify the biblical view of a successful pastorate. Kent began a mission church with great expectations for numerical growth, but after months of hard work he had a meager Sunday attendance. In deep depression, Kent expressed his bitterness to Barbara:

> What came forth was repugnant and offensive—truly mean. "Most people I know in the ministry are unhappy," I said. "They are failures in their own eyes. Mine as well." . . . I wasn't exaggerating the situation. Conversations over the years at pastor's conferences supported my thoughts. A few moments of personal exchange with a pastor almost invariably revealed immense hurt and self-doubt. Most pastors were unhappy with themselves and their work. And I secretly agreed with many of their self-assessments. . . . I went on: "How can I go on giving all that I have without seeing results, especially when others are?" I had been working day and night with no visible return. . . . If not that, then how should I measure my success?[16]

As the two talked, they became convinced that the problem was an undefined concept of success. What did it mean to be an effective pastor? Kent and Barbara made a covenant to search the Scriptures and learn what God had to say about success.

Measuring your success upon something other than numbers is certainly important for pastors and other ministers who are not leading large and growing programs. But clarifying one's priorities is especially important for those who lead numerically growing ministries. Achieving the culture's standard of success does not necessarily bring the satisfaction of achievement, as illustrated by astronaut Buzz Aldrin. Shortly after his return from the moon landing, Aldrin suffered an emotional breakdown. The collapse mystified many people. Why would a man who had reached the pinnacle of professional achievement and public acclaim break down? Aldrin later explained that his crisis had a simple explanation. He forgot that there was still life after the moon. Beyond the moon shot, he had no other objectives. In that personal vacuum, he collapsed.[17]

Pastors of large churches and staff members of large church programs have reached the culture's standard of success. Like

Aldrin, a minister can accept the call to a large church and still discover there's life after the move. Whether we serve in a small church or a large church, all of us need a standard of success beyond the proverbial "buildings, budgets, and baptisms." In *Priorities in Ministry*, Ernest Mosley points out:

> As you establish and clarify your priorities, you will . . . develop a measuring rod for success in ministry. . . . The degree to which we honor these life and work priorities is the measure of our success. And we don't have to ask someone to tell us whether we are successful or not. We don't depend on institutional growth or nongrowth factors as our primary measurement. The judgment comes from within, from a review of our priorities.[18]

FOUR STEPS TO MORE EFFECTIVE MINISTRY

Have you taken the time to define what a successful ministry means to you? Have you evaluated your present activities to see whether they are helping you fulfill your calling? Have you written out some plan to improve yourself as a minister? You will enjoy a more effective ministry if you commit the time to take four steps toward clarifying and achieving your personal ideals.

First, you need to prepare a written statement of your objectives. Objectives are timeless and immeasurable declarations of what you believe a minister has been called to be and do. Objectives transcend the circumstances of the church leader's life or his church field. The declarations are your beliefs regarding what any person in your position of ministry has been divinely commanded to be and do. We draw our statements of ideal ministry from the Bible.

Second, you need to examine ways you can fulfill your objectives in the church to which God has called you. In other words, after you have determined what you think is "successful" ministry, ask yourself what you are doing in your present situation that will make you successful. Which objectives would you claim as your strengths? Which ones need attention? What does the church and the community need from your leadership right now? Are there any activities that you should eliminate because they do not help you fulfill your mission?

Third, you need to set goals in relation to your statement of objectives. Goals are different from objectives. While objectives are timeless and cannot be measured, goals are dated and measurable. While objectives are declarations of what you believe every church leader in any setting should be doing, goals are statements of what you must do in your present church field.

Let me give you an example. Here's one of my objectives: "I will intercede in prayer for my congregation." That is a biblically-based declaration of what I believe every pastor in every church should be doing. Let's say that upon examining myself against that statement I realize that my prayer life would be more effective if I used a systematic plan to pray for every household on a regular basis. The following is a goal in relation to that evaluation: "I will pray for every household in my church once a quarter through the next church year." That is a dated, measurable declaration of what I believe God has called me to do in a specific church right now.

Finally, you need to make a plan of action for each goal that you set. In this way you move from wishful thinking to fulfillment. Consider the example above. What actions would I need to perform to pray for every household on the church roll quarterly? The following is an action plan for that goal: "(1) By July 1, purchase index cards and a card file; (2) by August 1, have the secretary type the names of all church member families on the cards, one family per card; (3) by October 1, set aside the first fifteen minutes Monday through Thursday, to pray over five to ten cards."

AWKWARD BEGINNINGS

"Thank you for providing this contest!" wrote one entrant. "I am finally able to enter a contest I am qualified for!" The letter was in reply to a contest sponsored by *Home Office Computing* magazine. The periodical was awarding a four thousand dollar custom-designed home office to the contestant who won the title of "The Most Disorganized Home Office." Applicants had to write, in fewer than two hundred words, why their workplace was the most chaotic. The magazine required a photograph of the offending office.

One contestant provided a hand-sketched picture of his office; he said he couldn't find his camera for the required photo. His application was dated February 1991. (The contest was held in 1993!) Another entrant wrote that he had prepared an essay but had misplaced it while working on his income taxes from two years back. Many others walked into the New York office of the magazine near closing time the day of the deadline. Some came to hand-deliver their last-minute applications, while others came to ask for extensions![19]

If you feel that you could win such a contest, then I imagine that my talk of objectives, goals, and action plans does not resonate with you. I would avoid the managerial terms if I could. But the words merely label the steps of a process we must all take—consciously or unconsciously—if we want to improve.

Think about it. Whenever we describe our priorities to search committees, aren't we taking step 1? Whenever we say to ourselves, *I've got to be more consistent in contacting church prospects!* or *Why can't I be more disciplined in my sermon preparation?* aren't we taking step 2? Whenever we begin some personal commitment, such as renewing daily devotionals, aren't we taking step 3? Whenever we engage in a long-term project, such as completing a seminary degree, aren't we taking step 4? In other words, we are always engaged in some process of personal improvement. The only question is, have we entered into the process consciously and deliberately, or have we engaged in it only unconsciously and by accident? Are we doing well or doing poorly at performing the four steps to effective ministry?

The four-step process described in this book is only a tool. Using any tool and starting any discipline is awkward at first. I experience this truth keenly every time I stand on the first tee of our community's golf course. There is nothing "natural" about golf for rookies like me! I am self-conscious about everything—my choice of club, my stance, my back swing, my down swing, the force of my swing, my follow-through, and so on. Experienced golfers tell me the awkwardness goes away, and I will become more at ease with my swing. I hope so! In the same way, you may find the four-step process of self-improvement unnatural and clumsy at first. Understand that the steps simply help you do intentionally what you have already been doing by accident.

Besides, many church leaders already use these techniques in leading their churches in long-range planning. Most of us know the benefits that come from helping a church develop a vision, set goals, and achieve victories. I have found that the process of evaluation and planning that has worked so well for the ministry can also benefit the minister.

IT'S WORTH YOUR WHILE!

Several years have passed since I first determined to work under a written mission statement. Each year since then I have set aside time in late July or early August for evaluation and planning. I examine my strengths and weaknesses against the mission statement and set goals for improvement. For example, I recently examined my work against my objective of administrating the church's affairs and found I needed work on moderating my church's business meetings. I set a goal of reading through *Robert's Rules of Order*, an article a month (riveting reading, you can be sure!).

By defining my priorities and identifying areas in which I want to grow, I can choose training events and materials more intelligently. I base my choice to attend a workshop, buy a book, or read an article in a periodical on how it helps me improve the performance of my objectives. When I am with other pastors, I find myself asking colleagues what things they are doing successfully in the areas in which I want improvement. The resulting conversation is always more exciting than idly chatting about last Sunday's attendance.

Of course, I do not live by my objectives perfectly, and I do not give every goal the attention it deserves. However, with my mission statement I have a mark toward which I can keep moving. A church leader who knows what well-done ministry looks like and who knows what it takes to have that kind of ministry will conclude his life's work with a sense of fulfillment.

Without a vision the minister perishes. *With a vision the minister flourishes!* In the chapters that follow, we will take the four steps toward having a flourishing service for Christ. Before continuing, however, make sure to complete the following activity.

ACTIVITY

Review the ten reasons why a church leader needs a personal mission statement. Which reason most convinced you that you need a "ministry manifesto" to improve your personal ministry? State the reason in your own words:

_____

_____

_____

_____

_____

_____

TWO

THE FIRST STEP: CREATE YOUR "MINISTRY MANIFESTO"

This is a job for Superman!

— Clark Kent

I N ONE OF THE "PEANUTS" EPISODES, little Linus is stuck out in an unkempt baseball field. Weeds rise above the boy's head. Linus is talking to himself. "I don't mind playing right field," he says. "I don't mind standing out here in weeds over my head—really I don't. I mean, if this is where I can do the team the most good, this is where I belong. . . . The only thing that bothers me is, I don't know if I'm facing the right way."[1]

Many of us are frustrated with our fields of ministry simply because we do not know if we are facing the right way! If we are to begin doing intentional ministry, we need to determine exactly what we want to accomplish as ministers. The first step toward more effective ministry, then, is to write a statement of our objectives—a "ministry manifesto." You need a written declaration of exactly how you want to be remembered as a minister.

Remember our definition of objectives. *Objectives are timeless and immeasurable declarations of what you believe any minister in your position has been divinely commanded to do.* The best statements are made by reviewing the Scriptures that relate to the work of the church leader and summarizing those Scriptures in a series of three to seven objectives.

For example, the following is an objective a pastor might write as part of his manifesto: "I will equip my congregation for works of service." That is a biblically-based declaration of what every pastor in every church should be doing. The following is a goal in relation to that objective: "This year I will become certified to begin a witness training course in my church." That is a dated, measurable declaration of what the pastor commits to do in a specific church right now.

Again, the following is an example of an objective that a minister of music might write as a part of his manifesto: "I will be a good administrator of the music program in the church I serve." That is a timeless and immeasurable declaration of the minister's intention. A goal toward fulfilling that intention could be: "By the end of this quarter I will inventory all the equipment belonging to the music ministry." That is a dated and measurable statement reflecting a need at a specific church in a specific point in its ministry. In the last chapter, we reviewed ten reasons why you should operate under a statement of objectives. In this chapter, we will note the *five features of well-prepared objectives.*

WRITTEN

First, objectives must be written. The process of writing it down takes what was once unexpressed or even undefined and exposes it to inspection and refinement. The process of writing forces you to be specific about the kind of minister God has called you to be.

There is an interesting instruction to future kings in Deuteronomy 17. After taking the throne, each king in his turn was to "write for himself" a copy of the law laid down through Moses. Furthermore, he must "read it all the days of his life so that he may learn to revere the Lord his God and follow carefully all the words of this law and these decrees and not consider himself better than his brothers and turn from the law to the right or to the left."[2] The divine law that guided both the king's national leadership and his personal conduct was in the possession of the priests, and the king could consult it at any time. But there was something convicting about the king's writing it down in his own script at the start of his leadership and reading it in the king's own handwriting throughout the years. Likewise, we ministers can know what God expects of us simply by turning to passages like Matthew 28:18–20 or Ephesians 4:11–13 or Colossians 1:28–29 or 1 Timothy 3:1–7. Still, there is something convicting about systematizing it in your own words and reading it in your own handwriting throughout the years.

UNIQUE CREATION

Second, a statement of objectives should be your personal creation. A minister could establish his mission by determining what congregations want in a church leader or by adopting a concept of ministry written by another minister or consultant. There is value in considering the expectations of our churches and the insights of other ministers who have hammered out a mission statement, but we should not begin there.

Determining What Congregations Want in a Church Leader

Do not begin defining your manifesto by determining what congregations want in a minister. Specialists in the field of clergy assessment call this the "status quo" procedure. Typical of this method is the *Readiness for Ministry* project conducted in the mid-1970s. In this project, laypersons, denominational leaders, pastors, and seminary professors from various religious bodies— not all of them Christian—were asked to specify the qualities they felt that clergy should have. The composite expectation was then offered as the criteria for assessing the strengths and weaknesses of clergy.[3]

Certainly, ministers cannot ignore the composite expectations identified in such a study. What is more important, ministers cannot dismiss the expectations of their local church and community. In another chapter, we will return to the issue of respecting the unique expectations and needs of your specific field of ministry.

Still, establishing the criteria against which you will measure your progress cannot begin with congregational preferences. As I said in the last chapter, the minister who has not determined his agenda quickly discovers many dominating people willing to do it for him! And while many expectations of the ministry are accurate, what Paul warned young Timothy about ought to make us mindful that we should not heed every preference of our congregations.

Paul wrote that Timothy must preach sound doctrine no matter what his congregation wanted to hear, for "the time will come when men will not put up with sound doctrine. Instead, to suit their own desires, they will gather around them a great number of teachers to say what their itching ears want to hear."[4]

With that warning in mind, pastors and the staff members who serve with them should not make the expectations of their churches the first place they turn for defining objectives.

Adopting a View of Ministry That Someone Else Has Developed

A second option available to ministers who want a written manifesto is to adopt a concept that another minister or consultant has already prepared. I have collected a number of ministry models over the years, such as the following five.

Probably the most famous model of ministry among Southern Baptists is one designed by Ernest Mosley. Mosley depicted the tasks of ministry by three interlocking circles. He labeled the circles, "proclaim," "care," and "lead" (see Fig. 2.1).

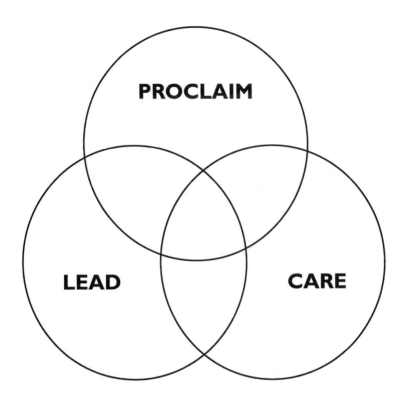

Figure 2.1: Mosley Ministry Model I

The church leader must *lead* the church in the achievement of its mission, *proclaim* the gospel, and *care* for the church's members and other persons in the community. In this model, the minister must not regard one task as more important than another task, and he or she must not perform one responsibility independently of the other two. Mosley called his model the "interlocking mutually supportive" view of ministry.[5] It is difficult to improve on such a balanced presentation of the responsibilities of the pastor and his associates on staff.

In his next book, *Priorities in Ministry*, Mosley proposed another diagram. He used six concentric circles to picture the priorities a church leader should have (see Fig. 2.2).

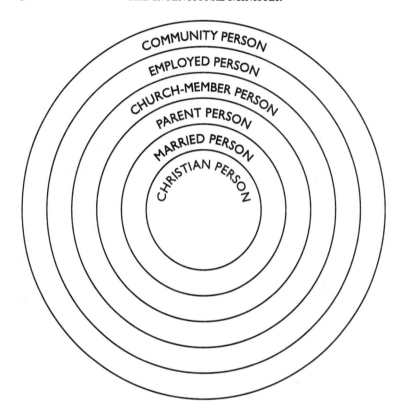

Figure 2.2: Mosley Ministry Model II

From the innermost circle to the outermost, Mosley labeled the spheres of responsibility: Christian person, married person, parent person, church member person, employed person, and community person. Referring to the center circle, "Christian person," he argued that the minister's life and work are held together by a relationship with Jesus Christ. Thus, if the minister gives inadequate attention to this priority relationship, no amount of investment in the outer priorities can cause him to achieve and maintain his potential. In fact, each circle builds upon the inner circles, so that success in the outer responsibilities depends upon success in the inner duties. Therefore, preoccupation with an outside circle must never take attention away from an inside circle.[6]

C. W. Brister, James L. Cooper, and J. David Fite suggested similar priorities for a minister in their book, *Beginning Your Ministry*. Like Mosley, they also regarded one's relationship with God as central. The authors pictured the priorities by means of four circles orbiting around a central circle.

They labeled the central circle "self centered in God." One's self-concept and one's corresponding relationship with God were regarded as primary. Around that priority orbited the other four circles, labeled "spouse," "children," "church," and "community."[7]

John Aker compared five ministry responsibilities to pins a juggler tries to keep aloft. The minister has the *pastoral* task of visitation, the *prophetic* task of preparing and preaching sermons, the *priestly* task of planning and conducting the services (worship services, weddings and funerals, and baptismal and communion services), the *professional* task of administration, and the *personal* task of developing one's spirituality.[8]

Kent and Barbara Hughes hoped to encourage ministers by affirming that success is within reach, regardless of the size or prominence of one's church. In *Liberating Ministry from the Success Syndrome*, they defined prosperous ministry by seven components: (1) obeying God's Word, (2) serving others in Christlikeness, (3) loving God with all one's heart, (4) believing God takes care of pastors and rewards their labors, (5) praying for oneself and others in imitation of Christ, (6) being holy—especially about sexual temptation, and (7) maintaining a positive attitude in any circumstance. [9]

A church leader could adopt one of these statements as his model for ministry. Again, as with the status quo criteria, ministers must not ignore the portrayals that others provide. The models reflect the wisdom that others have gained from constructing a statement of objectives. These models should not be the starting point as we define what our own calling involves, however. Have the writers left out some important aspect of ministry from their models? Have they placed emphasis where it should not be placed? Is there one objective that should take priority over the others? We will not know until we first declare our own convictions regarding what God has called ministers to be and do. You should use the models that others have prepared only to polish and refine your work. Your manifesto should be a unique creation.

TIMELESS

Third, objectives must be timeless, transcending the specifics of a local church or community. Your *goals* will reflect your perception of what your church and community need from you. But what do you perceive to be the things *any* minister in your position must be and do to hear Jesus say, "Well done"? Your manifesto should answer that question.

For example, imagine a minister of education who leads a Sunday School program that is out of space. He concludes that his objective is "to lead my church to start a second Sunday School." Such a statement fails to rise above the circumstances of his present church in its present need. The statement would be a start toward a fine *goal* but, since it is not timeless, it is not an *objective* by our definition.

If our hypothetical minister of education took a moment to clarify his mission, he would see that he recognizes the need to hold two Sunday Schools because one of his objectives is to develop effective small-group Bible studies. In his *present* church, the way he fulfills that objective is to relieve the over-crowding in the one Sunday School by starting a second meeting time. The objective, however, is one that he believes *any* minister of education would have on any church field—to develop small-group Bible studies.

But what about staff members who hold a combination of unrelated assignments—for example, "minister of music and senior adults" or "minister of education and youth"? Such positions have been created to meet the needs of a specific church. In fact, often the church expects the minister to give one assignment priority over the other, based on the local church's needs. Can ministers who hold these offices create manifestos that transcend the setting and needs of a particular church?

The men and women in places where unrelated assignments are combined can still create timeless mission statements. If you serve in such a position, imagine yourself back at seminary—but this time you are a guest lecturer, not a student. You are standing at the lectern in front of a room full of eager young men and women who are about to enter your very position in church staffs across the country. They will even have to give the same priority to one assignment over another, just as your church expects of you. You have been invited to speak on "The Ideal Minister of Music and Senior Adults"—or whatever office you hold. With rapt attention, the students wait with pens poised for your lecture. How would you summarize for them, in three to seven statements, your idea of a minister who does the job perfectly? Remember, they will not be serving at your particular church in your specific community. They will hold the same combination of assignments as you do, but some will serve large suburban congregations, some will serve smaller rural churches, some will lead church programs near university campuses, and some will direct ministries within inner cities. Regardless of the church and community, the description of their staff assignment will be much like yours. What would the ideal minister in your position look like, regardless of his church or setting?

COMPREHENSIVE

Fourth, the statement of objectives must be comprehensive. Every detail of ministerial work must have a place in your manifesto. I recommend that you try to keep your manifesto between three to seven divisions. This will ensure that your statement of objectives is comprehensive without becoming unmanageable.

Imagine a pastor who has declared that his mission in life is to be a relevant and persuasive communicator of God's Word. (That is not hard to imagine!) His passion is certainly commendable, but we could not say that it is comprehensive. What about personal counseling? And what about leadership of the church's mission and administration of the church's program? If these responsibilities are not part of the pastor's conscious mission statement, at worst he ignores them and at best he merely tolerates such work as a sideline to his "real" work of preaching.

Of course, each minister will give priority to certain tasks based on temperament, spiritual gifts, and setting. When forming an overarching concept of the ideal minister, however, the church leader must include everything that Christ expects. That leads to the fifth criterion of good objectives.

BIBLICALLY-BASED

The objectives of ministers must be biblically-based. There ought to be scriptural justification for each statement in your manifesto. And there ought to be a place in your manifesto for everything that the inspired writers presented as part of the office of the minister.

The oversight of a church requires attention to the following areas, whether that oversight is the responsibility of one minister or a team of ministers. The objectives include *demonstration*—being an example of doctrinal and ethical soundness; *proclamation*—making the Scriptures clear and applicable to the congregation; *administration*—managing the church's affairs; *delegation*—equipping believers to minister; and *supplication*—interceding in prayer for the members.

Demonstration

First, God wants the pastor and his staff to demonstrate authentic Christian living. In an April 1988 evening newscast, film footage was shown from a bizarre skydiving accident. The jump was photographed by a man who was himself an experienced sky diver. He filmed skydivers jumping out of an airplane and opening their parachutes above him. As the last chute opened, the television picture began spinning wildly—right, left, up and down. It was then that the newscast anchor reported that the photographer had fallen to his death, having jumped without a parachute. He had been so busy focusing on the experience of others that he failed to give attention to his own skydiving experience.

Pastors and staff persons can suffer the same tragedy. We can focus on monitoring the relationship that others have with Christ but fail to give attention to our own relationship with the Lord. "Oh what aggravated misery is this," wrote the Puritan Divine Richard Baxter, "to perish in the midst of plenty!—to famish with the bread of life in our hands, while we offer it to others."[10]

Paul described the purity God expects from church leaders: a minister must "watch" his "life and doctrine closely."[11] Our motto should be, "I beat my body and make it my slave so that after I have preached to others, I myself will not be disqualified for the prize."[12]

The men and women who serve on a church staff live this holy lifestyle with the consciousness that they set the example for the congregation. Ministers are to "set an example for the believers in speech, in life, in love, in faith and in purity."[13] Simon Peter appealed to pastors to shepherd God's flock not by lording it over believers, but by "being examples to the flock."[14] Paul commanded the church to "join with others in following my example, brothers, and take note of those who live according to the pattern we gave you."[15]

Proclamation

The second task God expects of church leaders is proclamation. The apostles regarded the "ministry of the Word" as so central to their work that they refused to allow anything to dilute their attention to it.[16] Therefore, the church leader must be "able to teach" in a way that is both gentle and authoritative.[17] In his teaching, he must "show integrity, seriousness and soundness of speech that cannot be condemned."[18]

In what ways do pastors and staff members give attention to the ministry of the Word? Proclamation certainly includes the pastor's job of preaching. Paul solemnly charged Timothy to "preach the Word"—a charge made in the presence of no less than "God and of Christ Jesus, who will judge the living and the dead, and in view of his appearing and his kingdom."[19] God calls pastors to proclaim the Word of God from the pulpit.

To that end, we pastors must train our churches and discipline ourselves to guard our preparation for standing behind what the old preachers called *the sacred desk*. Floyd Shafer made the same point with the subtlety of a pile driver in an old *Christianity Today* article:

> Fling him [the pastor] into his office, tear the *office* sign from the door and nail on the sign, *study*. Take him off the mailing list, lock him up with his books—and get him all kinds of books—and his typewriter and his Bible. . . . Force him to be the one man in our surfeited communities who knows about God. . . . Set a time clock on him that would imprison him with thought and writing about God for forty hours a week. Shut his garrulous mouth spouting remarks and stop his tongue always tripping lightly over everything non-essential. Bend his knees to the lonesome valley, and fire him from the PTA and cancel his country club membership. Rip out his telephone, burn his ecclesiastical success sheets, refuse his glad hand, put water in the gas tank of his community buggy and compel him to be a minister of the word.[20]

Pastors must also bring God's Word to bear on individual's lives in more intimate settings—visiting in a home, sitting by a hospital bed, counseling one-on-one in the pastor's office. Paul demonstrated that the church leader must "preach anything that would be helpful" both "publicly and from house to house."[21]

Some commentators believe that Paul was referring to house churches here, not personal visitation. In other words, these commentators believe Paul was reminding the Ephesian elders that he preached both in the public square and in the Christian assemblies that met in houses.

However, I am persuaded that the phrase "from house to house" in Acts 20:20 is a reference to Paul's habit of visiting individuals and families. When Paul complained about idle young widows in 1 Timothy 5:13, he said that they were wasting their time going "from house to house"—not likely a reference to attending the meetings of various house churches. In 1554, John Calvin wrote of this text from Acts:

> Christ did not ordain pastors on the principle that they only teach the Church in a general way on the public platform, but that they also care for the individual sheep, bring back the wandering and scattered to the fold, bind up those broken and crippled, heal the sick, support the frail and weak; for general teaching will often have a cold reception, unless it is helped by advice given in private. Accordingly there is no excuse for the negligence of those who, after holding one meeting, live for the rest of the time free from care, as if they have discharged their duty. It is as if their voices were shut up in the sanctuary, since they become completely dumb as soon as they come out of it.[22]

In other words, the pastor must observe the biblical command to "correct, rebuke and encourage"[23] by a hospital bed, in a lost person's living room, or in a counseling session—not just in the pulpit. John Henry Jowett reminded seminary students in 1912 that, in moving from the pulpit to the individual, "There is a change of sphere but no change of mission. . . . His audience is smaller, his business is the same."[24] In my own manifesto, I have grouped personal visitation, one-on-one counseling, and preaching together under one objective.

But proclamation also includes music, and the minister of music has been called to fulfill this objective. Simon Peter called Christians "a royal priesthood" that exists to "declare the praises of him who called you out of darkness into his wonderful light."[25] Paul urged the Colossian congregation to "let the word of Christ dwell. . . richly" in them as they taught each other by means of "psalms, hymns and spiritual songs."[26] Music can be used to proclaim the congregation's praise to God and to proclaim God's Word to the congregation. God calls music ministers to lead choirs and congregations in this work.

The objective of proclamation is also fulfilled by ministers in charge of the education program, the counseling program, and evangelism ministries. These persons direct ministries where the message of God is shared in small groups and in one-on-one settings.

Because of this priority on sharing the Word of God with others, the minister must nurture a *personal devotion* to the Word. Paul told Titus that only a person who held "firmly to the trustworthy message as it has been taught" can both encourage believers and refute those who attack the faith.[27]

Besides a personal devotion to the Word, the minister must develop a *professional discipline* in the Word. Every minister's desire must be to present himself "as one approved, a workman who does not need to be ashamed and who correctly handles the word of truth."[28]

Administration

A third objective expected of ministry leaders is administration. Unfortunately, some church leaders neglect this task when writing their manifestos because they think of administration as dry and unspiritual. At best, these ministers will regard this task as a necessary nuisance that they must endure so that the "real" work of ministry can be sustained. In fact, the article on "spirituality" in the *Evangelical Dictionary of Theology* lists the current interest in administration among church leaders as one of the main reasons for the "dearth of spiritual leadership and direction in the evangelical world."[29]

Far from regarding such work as unspiritual, Paul included it among his lists of spiritual gifts. In the list of gifted persons in 1 Corinthians, Paul included the *kuberneseis*—translated in the New International Version as "those with gifts of administration."[30] The word was originally used of those who piloted ships and had about it the idea of skillful directing. In Paul's list of gifted persons in Romans, he included the *proistamenos*—those having leadership.[31]

The use of *proistamenos* occurs repeatedly. In 1 Timothy, the word was used to name those who "direct the affairs" of the church, and a variant of the word was used to describe the overseer who must know how "to manage" his own household else he will not be fit to take care of the household of faith. The word was also used in 1 Thessalonians of those "who are over" the congregation in the Lord.[32]

The ministry leader must therefore develop competence in practical matters of church operation, such as church finances, long-range and short-range planning, and managing staff and volunteers. According to the Bible, such work does not *stifle* the Spirit; such work is *empowered* by the Spirit!

Delegation

Fourth, the church leader must delegate the work of ministry to his people, providing them with the training and motivation needed. I've met ministers like the following man, described in a newspaper article:

> In performing a wedding this minister . . . donned his coveralls to clear the pews; disappeared for a quick change before coming to the organ bench to play the prelude; hurried back to march out with the groom; performed the ceremony; sang the closing prayer; raced to the vestibule, asking the people to remain in their places until he arrived there; and with one hand greeting the attenders and another pointing guests to the visitors' registry, he placed one free foot in the church bell rope and tolled the bell![33]

When asked by the reporter why he didn't get someone to help him, he replied that he would rather do it all himself. Perhaps he had found, as many of us also have, that he could do the jobs better by himself than by entrusting them to volunteers. However, part of our job is to equip our congregations to join us in the work of the ministry. Can we say that a program has been well done by biblical standards if it runs smoothly but no lay persons have been trained to serve?

Paul instructed Timothy to "entrust to reliable men" the teaching Timothy heard from Paul.[34] Pastors and the staff members who help them are God's gifts to the local church to "prepare God's people for works of service."[35] Every believer belongs to the "royal priesthood" in which he uses "whatever gift he has received to serve others, faithfully administering God's grace in its various forms."[36]

God has called the pastor and his staff to equip the members to administrate the gifts God has given them so that the church might function smoothly. We should use sermons, seminars, training courses, and opportunities for service to prepare every believer for involvement in the mission of the church.

Supplication

Finally, the biblical writers described, and demonstrated, the ministry task of intercession. Of course, ordained ministers are not the exclusive mediators to God on behalf of our people. On the other hand, Scripture regards prayer as a special function of the minister. The apostles refused to allow anything to interfere with their responsibility to pray.[37] James commanded the sick to "call the elders of the church to pray" over them.[38] Curtis Vaughn said that the elders in this verse are identifiable with pastors and "are mentioned specifically because they are the persons within the congregation who above all others should be men of prayer. But alas! this is not always true."[39]

Many New Testament letters include intercessory prayers on behalf of the churches. Consider this opening prayer of the Ephesian letter (1:16–19):

> I have not stopped giving thanks for you, remembering you in my prayers. I keep asking that the God of our Lord Jesus Christ, the glorious Father, may give you the Spirit of wisdom and revelation, so that you may know him better. I pray also that the eyes of your heart may be enlightened in order that you may know the hope to which he has called you, the riches of his glorious inheritance in the saints, and his incomparably great power for us who believe.

Consider this prayer, from the opening verses of Paul's letter to the Philippians (1:9–11):

> And this is my prayer: that your love may abound more and more in knowledge and depth of insight, so that you may be able to discern what is best and may be pure and blameless until the day of Christ, filled with the fruit of righteousness that comes through Jesus Christ—to the glory and praise of God.

Again, imagine the pastoral heart behind this prayer, penned by the anonymous author of Hebrews (13:20–21):

> May the God of peace, who through the blood of the eternal covenant brought back from the dead our Lord Jesus, that great Shepherd of the sheep, equip you with everything good for doing his will, and may he work in us what is pleasing to him, through Jesus Christ, to whom be glory for ever and ever. Amen.

Other pastoral prayers on behalf of the churches can be found in Ephesians 3:14–21; Philippians 1:3–6; Colossians 1:9–12; 1 Thessalonians 1:2–3; 3:11–13; 2 Thessalonians 1:11–12; 2:16–17; 3:5; 3:16. I have been trying to memorize some of these scriptural intercessions for use in my morning prayer routine.

My favorite example of pastoral praying is Epaphras. Paul reported to the Colossians that Epaphras was "always wrestling in prayer" for them.[40] We do not know for sure whether Epaphras was the pastor of the Colossian congregation. We read only that he was "a faithful minister of Christ" through whom the Colossians had come to believe.[41] But he certainly maintained a pastoral concern for those he led to Christ.

And Paul wrote that he often observed Epaphras "wrestling" in prayer on their behalf. The Greek word is *agonizomenos*—if you pronounce it you will hear the word "agony."

When I reflect on Epaphras, his example always convicts me. If I am not careful, my intercession will often degenerate into a few tired sentences between yawns and sips of coffee as I start my work day. I could hardly describe that as agonized wrestling against principalities and powers on behalf of my congregation!

Richard Foster said it best. He said that if we love people, we will desire far more than is within our ability to give them, and that will lead us to prayer.[42] Church leaders cannot claim to have a comprehensive and biblically-based mission statement if they do not include the task of intercession.

THIS IS THE WEDDING REHEARSAL!

The pastor and his staff must perform this five-fold calling of demonstration, proclamation, administration, delegation, and supplication with the aim of presenting mature disciples to Christ upon His return. In *What Really Matters in Ministry*, Darius Salter said, "A bride properly attired and prepared for the Lamb, ready to stand before him in her wedding garment, is the ultimate goal of ministry. Anything short of that is absolute failure."[43] Christ will judge our stewardship, in part, based on the maturity of the people for whom we were responsible.

We can sense the seriousness with which first-century church leaders took this judgment by reading their Spirit-inspired comments in the Bible. The writer of Hebrews urged his readers to obey their leaders because they "keep watch over you as men who must give an account."[44]

We translate "keep watch" from the Greek word *agrupnousin*. The word is a combination of *agreuo*—to chase, and *hupnos*—to sleep. It literally means "chasing sleep, sleeplessness." It is used in the New Testament to mean that wakefulness that comes from intently watching over something. It has the idea of a watchman who keeps watch over the camp, or the idea of a doctor staying by the bedside of a critically-ill patient. The New English Bible translates the phrase—"they are tireless in their concern for you."

The writer then adds, "as men who must give an account." Commentators differ on whether the writer intended to say that church leaders must account for how they watched or for what they saw. I have always understood that verse to mean that on the day of reckoning, I will have to account for the faithfulness with which I watched over the people I serve.

Paul also maintained that he performed his labors under an awareness that Christ would examine the maturity of Paul's converts. He told the Thessalonians that they were his "crown," in which he would "glory in the presence of our Lord Jesus when he comes."[45] He urged the Philippians to live blameless lives "in order that I may boast on the day of Christ that I did not run or labor for nothing."[46] He reminded the Corinthians, "You yourselves are our letter [of recommendation], written on our hearts, known and read by everybody. You show that you are a letter from Christ, the result of our ministry. . . ."[47] In other words, a minister's real resume, "known and read by everybody," is written by the collective lifestyle of the people he or she has been serving! F. F. Bruce said of Paul:

> Above all, he hopes that when he gives a final account of his apostolic stewardship to the Lord who commissioned him he will need to do no more than point to his converts and have the quality of his service judged by their faith and life.[48]

Like Paul, pastors and their staff members must work under the awareness that God will judge their stewardship not simply by the quality of their labors but also by the quality of their church members.

SAMPLE MANIFESTOS

By completing the activity at the end of this chapter, you will have a ministry manifesto that fulfills the criteria of well-prepared mission statements—written, timeless, comprehensive, and biblically-based. The following are sample statements that ministers in various positions could have written.

A pastor:

1. I will be an example of authentic Christian living.

2. Both publicly and privately, I will make the Scriptures clear and applicable to God's people.

3. I will be a good manager of church matters.

4. I will train and motivate God's people to do the work of ministry.

5. I will intercede in prayer for God's people.

An associate pastor:

1. I will demonstrate what it means to be a victorious Christian in all circumstances

2. I will support my pastor's pulpit ministry by handling other pastoral duties competently.

3. I will see that the administrative duties for which I am responsible are done well.

4. I will help the deacons be effective in the work of pastoral ministry.

5. I will be an intercessor for God's people.

A minister of music:

1. I will be the kind of Christian that others could follow.

2. I will work with my pastor to prepare worship services that bring people into God's presence and open their hearts to hear the Word of God.

3. I will administrate an efficient music program.

4. I will see that the volunteer and paid workers in my music ministry are properly trained, supervised, motivated, and thanked.

5. Through prayer I will make the throne of God familiar territory to me before I try to direct people to it on Sundays.

A minister to students:

1. I will set the example of discipleship for the students I serve.

2. I will see that every lesson brought to a youth meeting, whether by me or by a volunteer worker or by a guest speaker, is both biblical and relevant.

3. I will be an effective administrator of the program I lead, under the supervision of my pastor.

4. I will interpret the mission of my church to the students and represent the interests of the students to my church.

5. I will be an effective discipler of the students and the adults who influence them.

6. I will be an intercessor for the students and the adults who influence them.

Of course, the above statements are simply examples. Creating a manifesto of your own will be more meaningful to you than borrowing someone else's. The following activity will help you prepare a statement of objectives that is unique to your understanding of the minister's work.

ACTIVITY

On the following pages, you will find cards of selected Scriptures that address the role of the minister. Copy these pages and clip the cards. Remove any cards that do not address your position. Then arrange the remaining cards into stacks of similarity. In other words, arrange the cards that address the role of teaching into one stack and gather the texts that speak to the role of praying into another stack. If you have other Scriptures that have challenged you in the performance of your ministry, add them.

measurable declarations of what any minister in your position should be and do, regardless of the church or the community. Now, write one objective for each stack of Scripture cards. Remember that your objectives must be timeless and iml suggest you keep the number of your objectives between three and seven.

After you have written your objectives, make sure that your objectives cover every task to which Christ has called you. Skim through the five tasks that were described in this chapter and see if your objectives include these functions. (The tasks were *demonstration, proclamation, administration, delegation, and supplication.*) Let someone critique your manifesto against the definition in this chapter—a marriage partner, a support group, or a staff supervisor. Make sure that your mission statement summarizes your concept of well-done ministry before you continue in this book.

"For this reason, since the day we heard about you, we have not stopped praying for you and asking God to fill you with the knowledge of his will through all spiritual wisdom and understanding. And we pray this in order that you may live a life worthy of the Lord and may please him in every way." (Col. 1:9–10)	"In the presence of God and of Christ Jesus, who will judge the living and the dead, and in view of his appearing and his kingdom, I give you this charge: Preach the Word; be prepared in season and out of season; correct, rebuke and encourage—with great patience and careful instruction." (2 Tim. 4:1–2)
"But you, keep your head in all situations, endure hardship." (2 Tim. 4:5)	"Is any one of you sick? He should call the elders of the church to pray over him and anoint him with oil in the name of the Lord." (Jas. 5:14)
"But you . . . do the work of an evangelist." (2 Tim. 4:5)	"Now this is our boast: Our conscience testifies that we have conducted ourselves in the world, and especially in our relations with you, in the holiness and sincerity that are from God." (2 Cor. 1:12)
"It was he who gave some to be . . . pastors and teachers, to prepare God's people for works of service, so that the body of Christ may be built up." (Eph. 4:11–12)	"And in the church God has appointed . . . those with gifts of administration." (1 Cor. 12:28)

"And the things you have heard me say in the presence of many witnesses entrust to reliable men who will also be qualified to teach others." (2 Tim. 2:2)	"My message and my preaching were not with wise and persuasive words, but with a demonstration of the Spirit's power, so that your faith might not rest on men's wisdom, but on God's power."(1 Cor. 2:4–5)
"We have different gifts, according to the grace given us. If a man's gift is . . . leadership, let him govern diligently." (Rom. 12:6 and 8)	". . . your leaders . . . keep watch over you as men who must give an account." (Heb. 13:17)
"We were gentle among you, like a mother caring for her little children. We loved you so much that we were delighted to share with you not only the gospel of God but our lives as well, because you had become so dear to us." (1 Thess. 2:7–8)	"We preach Christ crucified." (1 Cor. 1:23)
"For you know that we dealt with each of you as a father deals with his own children, encouraging, comforting and urging you to live lives worthy of God, who calls you into his kingdom and glory." (1 Thess. 2:11–12)	"You know that I have not hesitated to preach anything that would be helpful to you but have taught you *publicly.*" (*Acts 20:20, emphasis added*)

" You know that I have not hesitated to preach anything that would be helpful to you but have taught you . . . *from house to house.*" (Acts 20:20, emphasis added)	"Guard the good deposit that was entrusted to you—guard it with the help of the Holy Spirit who lives in us." (2 Tim. 1:14)
"You must teach what is in accord with sound doctrine." (Titus 2:1)	"We always thank God for all of you, mentioning you in our prayers. We continually remember before our God and Father your work produced by faith, your labor prompted by love, and your endurance inspired by hope in our Lord Jesus Christ." (1 Thess. 1:2–3)
"Encourage and rebuke with all authority. Do not let anyone despise you." (Titus 2:15)	"Those [elders] who sin are to be rebuked publicly, so that the others may take warning." (1 Tim. 5:20)
"Epaphras, who is one of you and a servant of Christ Jesus . . . is always wrestling in prayer for you, that you may stand firm in all the will of God, mature and fully assured." (Col. 4:12)	"We constantly pray for you, that our God may count you worthy of his calling, and that by his power he may fulfill every good purpose of yours and every act prompted by your faith. We pray this so that the name of our Lord Jesus may be glorified in you, and you in him, according to the grace of our God and the Lord Jesus Christ." (2 Thess. 1:11–12)

"The elders who *direct the affairs of the church* well are worthy of double honor, especially those whose work is preaching and teaching." (1 Tim. 5:17, emphasis added)	"For we do not preach ourselves, but Jesus Christ as Lord, and ourselves as your servants for Jesus' sake." (2 Cor. 4:5)
"The elders who direct the affairs of the church well are worthy of double honor, especially those whose work is *preaching and teaching*." (1 Tim. 5:17, emphasis added)	"In everything set them an example by doing what is good" (Titus 2:7)
"And the Lord's servant must not quarrel; instead, he must be kind to everyone, able to teach, not resentful. Those who oppose him he must gently instruct, in the hope that God will grant them repentance leading them to a knowledge of the truth, and that they will come to their senses and escape from the trap of the devil, who has taken them captive to do his will." (2 Tim. 2:24–26)	"In your teaching show integrity, seriousness and soundness of speech that cannot be condemned, so that those who oppose you may be ashamed because they have nothing bad to say about us." (Titus 2:7–8)
"Train yourself to be godly." (1 Tim. 4:7)	"May the Lord make your love increase and overflow for each other and for everyone else, just as ours does for you. May he strengthen your hearts so that you will be blameless and holy in the presence of our God and Father when our Lord Jesus comes with all his holy ones." (1 Thess. 3:12–13)

"Do your best to present yourself to God as one approved, a workman who does not need to be ashamed and who correctly handles the word of truth." (2 Tim. 2:15)	"Devote yourself to the public reading of Scripture, to preaching and to teaching." (1 Tim. 4:13)
"Join with others in following my example, brothers, and take note of those who live according to the pattern we gave you." (Phil. 3:17)	"Watch your life and doctrine closely. Persevere in them, because if you do, you will save both yourself and your hearers." (1 Tim. 4:16)
"It would not be right for us to neglect the ministry of the word of God in order to wait on tables. Brothers, choose seven men from among you who are known to be full of the Spirit and wisdom. We will turn this responsibility over to them and will give our attention to *prayer.*" (Acts 6:1–4, emphasis added)	"An elder must be blameless, the husband of but one wife, a man whose children believe and are not open to th charge of being wild and disobedient. Since an overseer is entrusted with God's work, he must be blameless—not overbearing, not quick—tempered, not given to much worse, not violent, not pursuing dishonest gain. Rather he must be hospitable, one who loves what is good, who is self-controlled, upright, holy and disciplined. He must hold firmly to the trustworthy message as it has been taught, so that he can encourage others by sound doctrine and refute those who oppose it." (Titus 1:6–9)
"It would not be right for us to neglect the ministry of the word of God in order to wait on tables. Brothers, choose seven men from among you who are known to be full of the Spirit and wisdom. We will turn this responsibility over to them and will give our attention to . . . *the ministry of the word.*" (Acts 6:2–4, emphasis added)	

"Remember your leaders, who spoke the word of God to you. Consider the outcome of their way of life and imitate their faith." (Heb. 13:7)	"Not that we lord it over your faith, but we work with you for your joy. . . ." (2 Cor. 1:24)
"Whatever you have learned or received or heard from me, or seen in me—put it into practice." (Phil. 4:9)	"And this is my prayer: that your love may abound more and more in knowledge and depth of insight, so that you may be able to discern what is best and may be pure and blameless until the day of Christ, filled with the fruit of righteousness that comes through Jesus Christ—to the glory and praise of God." (Phil. 1:9–11)
"We who teach will be judged more strictly." (Jas. 3:1)	"Set an example for the believers in speech, in life, in love, in faith and in purity." (1 Tim. 4:12)
"I beat my body and make it my slave so that after I have preached to others, I myself will not be disqualified for the prize." (1 Cor. 9:27)	"May our Lord Jesus Christ himself and God our Father, who loved us and by his grace gave us eternal encouragement and good hope, encourage your hearts and strengthen you in every good deed and word." (2 Thess. 2:16–17)

"Now may the Lord of peace himself give you peace at all times and in every way. The Lord be with all of you." (2 Thess. 3:16)	"Jesus said, 'Feed my sheep.'" (John 21:17)
"We have different gifts, according to the grace given us. If a man's gift is . . . leadership, let him govern diligently." (Rom. 12:6, 8)	The elder "must hold firmly to the trustworthy message as it has been taught, so that he can encourage others by sound doctrine and refute those who oppose it." (Titus 1:9)
"May the Lord direct your hearts into God's love and Christ's perseverance." (2 Thess. 3:5)	"If anyone does not know how to manage his own family, how can he take care of God's church?" (1 Tim. 3:5)
"May the God of peace, who through the blood of the eternal covenant brought back from the dead our Lord Jesus, that great Shepherd of the sheep, equip you with everything good for doing his will, and may he work in us what is pleasing to him, through Jesus Christ, to whom be glory for ever and ever. Amen." (Heb. 13:20–21)	"But you, man of God, . . . pursue righteousness, godliness, faith, love, endurance and gentleness. Fight the good fight of the faith. Take hold of the eternal life to which you were called when you made your good confession in the presence of many witnesses." (1 Tim. 6:11–12)

"I have not stopped giving thanks for you, remembering you in my prayers. I keep asking that the God of our Lord Jesus Christ, the glorious Father, may give you the Spirit of wisdom and revelation, so that you may know him better. I pray also that the eyes of your heart may be enlightened in order that you may know the hope to which he has called you, the riches of his glorious inheritance in the saints, and his incomparably great power for us who believe." (Eph. 1:16–19)	"Be shepherds of God's flock that is under your care, serving as overseers—not because you must, but because you are willing, as God wants you to be; not greedy for money, but eager to serve; not lording it over those entrusted to you, but being examples to the flock." (1 Pet. 5:2–3)

THREE

THE SECOND STEP:
A PERSONAL CHECKUP

Do not neglect your gift.

—The Apostle Paul
1 Timothy 4:14

I N ONE OF THE CONGREGATIONS I served, an Olympic weight lifter and his young family joined our church. He had competed in the 1992 summer games in Barcelona just weeks before joining our fellowship. I once again was reminded of the intense examination Olympic athletes endure to improve their performance.

A weekly newsmagazine reported that during training, Olympic hopefuls willingly subject themselves to various inspections, depending on the event.[1] Some are photographed at 2000 frames a second to scrutinize their work frame by frame. Some run a video image of their performance through a computer program designed to detect flaws. Others even measure the number of breaths the lungs take and the number of beats the heart makes during their event. At the U.S. Swimming Federation's International Center for Aquatic Research in Colorado Springs, coaches have tested over ten thousand swimmers on a swimming treadmill called a flume. The flume is a tiny tank in which the athlete swims against a mechanically generated current. The swimmer wears a mouthpiece by which oxygen intake is measured and strokes are filmed.

So-called "biomechanics experts" examine the minutest movements. For example, they advised freestyle swimmer Matt Biondi to keep his wrist cocked for one-half second longer at the end of each stroke to maximize his propulsion. These researchers use infrared lasers, force plates, and computer-enhanced video images to capture every type of athletic movement for intense inspection—the twist of a high diver, the leap of a runner at the hurdle, the lunge of a weight lifter like my friend.

The performances of Olympic hopefuls are rehearsed and reviewed repeatedly as coaches and athletes try to strike out the tiniest flaw that would deny our country a medal. In the same manner, an intentional minister submits to personal reviews with that kind of intensity, not for a country but for a kingdom.

Of course, self-examination would be pointless without an explicit standard. After completing the activity at the end of chapter 2, you should have a "yardstick" by which to measure your ministry. Your mission statement is a written declaration of what you believe God expects of *any* minister in your position. You are not just any minister, though. You serve in a one-of-a-kind place and you have a one-of-a-kind mix of abilities, interests, and opportunities.

Have you succeeded in being all that God would want you to be in the specific place to which He has called you? That is the question you must ask in the second step toward becoming an intentional minister. Holding your manifesto in one hand and a mirror in the other, you must now perform a personal checkup.

How should you perform checkups for personal and professional improvement? Your examination should include the following elements: imagination, prayer, claiming your own personal gifts, inviting feedback from those you serve, noting the interests of your church and the larger Christian fellowship, and being aware of the urgent needs of the community.

IMAGINATION

Soon after the completion of Disney World, someone said, "Isn't it too bad that Walt Disney didn't live to see this?" An executive replied, "What do you mean? He did see it—that's why it's here." Imagination is a powerful force. In *Beginning Your Ministry,* the authors suggest that imagination is a minister's first step in designing a plan for personal and professional growth. They write:

> The late Harry Emerson Fosdick observed that "great living starts with a picture held in some person's imagination of what he would like to be." . . . Imagine what you will be in five or ten years. Verbalize what you want to look back on in your life and ministry after twenty years.[2]

Of course, the effective minister will move beyond envisioning where he wants to be and activate an aggressive plan to get there. Imagination alone can result in a sort of Walter Mitty syndrome. James Thurbur created this hapless character in the 1940s. The daydreaming Mitty was an instant hit—in fact, the storyline was made into a popular film in 1947 with Danny Kaye in the leading role in "The Secret Life of Walter Mitty." Poor Mitty escaped the boredom of his life by daydreaming that he was the hero of his own adventures. It was only a temporary escape, though. Returning from his imaginary adventures, Mitty acquiesced to the drudgery that was his life. We can end up with a starring role in our own "Secret Life of Reverend Mitty" if our planning goes no further than wishful thinking.

While the process of self-improvement does not end with imagination, it certainly begins there. In the best-selling *The Seven Habits of Highly Effective People,* Stephen Covey explained that highly effective people realize that things are determined mentally before they are determined physically. That is, who one becomes and what one accomplishes is often decided in the heart before being established in experience.

Ineffective people passively permit old habits, other people, and environmental conditions to dictate that first creation—

often unconsciously. They make truce with the inner voices of the past and present, voices that surround them saying, "You can't. . . . You're not capable. . . . You aren't ready yet. . . . You don't have the resources. . . . The circumstances are too over-whelming. . . ." and so on. Unfortunately, those reactions create self-fulfilling prophecies in which the person finds that he really couldn't, that he really wasn't capable, that he in fact was not prepared enough, that the circumstances were actually too insurmountable, and so on.

On the other hand, effective people take control of the mental picture of what they want to be and do. Intentional ministers take control of what they want to accomplish in their ministries in light of their written mission statements. Our upbringing, our level of ministerial training, our availability to good mentors, and the environment of our churches should not determine what kind of ministers we will be. We should determine what we must become based on our divine calling. Personal and professional improvement begins by defining your concept of ideal ministry and then imagining what you would look like and act like if you were fulfilling that concept.

PRAYER

Activate your imagination in the context of prayerful medita-tion. The wise man wrote, "Commit to the Lord whatever you do, and your plans will succeed."[3] The Amplified Bible para-phrases the verse, "Roll your works upon the Lord (commit and trust them wholly to Him; He will cause your thoughts to become agreeable to His will, and) so shall your plans be established and succeed." The imperative is from the Hebrew word *galal*, which means to roll away or remove. The word evokes the image of relinquishing ownership of one's plans and the anxiety that goes with it. In so doing, God will cause our thoughts to become agreeable to His thoughts and in that way our plans will stand.

James said that without this feature our planning would be presumptuous. He wrote:

> Now listen, you who say, "Today or tomorrow we will go to this or that city, spend a year there, carry on business and make money." Why, you do not even know what will happen tomorrow. . . . Instead, you ought to say, "If it is the Lord's will, we will live and do this or that."[4]

Ask the Father to take your dreamings and shape them to conform to His desires! We should not hesitate to confess to Him even those desires that are driven by improper motives. There is a line in a familiar praise chorus that goes, "The One who knows me best loves me most." He knows our hearts, and we can be sure that He will respond gently when we confess whatever impurities are there. At the throne, God will either purify or replace our plans to bring them into line with His desires.

Replacing Our Desires

As we roll our plans upon Him and relinquish ownership of them, He may trade newer, better desires for our old, improper dreams. For example, He may replace a pastor's desire for a larger congregation with a passion to stay and restore hope to a smaller, struggling congregation.

Larry Lewis, president of the SBC Home Mission Board, remembers the time he served a growing congregation in Ohio. The pastor of a smaller church in Columbus invited him to preach revival services. The church was located in an almost totally Jewish community and growth had been difficult to produce. By contrast, Lewis's church was growing rapidly in a new housing area, and he enjoyed some recognition from its success. After a week-long revival that produced very meager tangible results, Lewis asked his friend, "Why don't you quit here and move to a more receptive area—perhaps a growing suburb?" The pastor replied, "There's a work here that needs to be done. There are people here who need to be reached."

Lewis never forgot that response. As president of the Home Mission Board, he has seen many other examples of this type of commitment—pastors, church planters, center workers, language missionaries, and others who are willing to labor where the potential seems small. Lewis warns, "We must be careful about defining success in terms of numbers. God measures success in terms of faithfulness. *God wants followers who will stick with tough situations until the purposes of God are fulfilled there.*[5]

Naturally, some would regard such tough situations as dead ends, both in terms of personal fulfillment and professional recognition. According to Darius Salter, efforts at discouraging us from staying in disappointing fields are like Simon Peter's efforts at discouraging Jesus from going to the cross.[6] Peter's words drew Jesus's most vehement response: "Out of my sight, Satan!" What looked to Simon Peter as absolute failure was the Father's means of redemption. Therefore, Jesus committed to stay within the Father's will. What appears to our own colleagues and relatives as a dead end could play some part in the Father's great plan of redeeming the world. Salter writes, "Everything done in the church needs to be examined and evaluated through a Christological lens. . . . At the apex of the cross all production must pass inspection."[7]

"Throw me something, mister!" That's the call heard at Mardi Gras parades each spring in south Louisiana. While I pastored a church there, I took my three-year-old to one of the parades in a small town. He sat on my shoulders, stuck out his little chubby hand, and said in an eager toddler voice, "Throw me something, mister!" From the floats, people in bright costumes and painted faces threw candy and doubloons and trinkets into the crowd. With hands raised, the crowds elbowed and shoved each other to get at the loot. They even stomped on the hands of people foolish enough to reach down to pick up fallen coins!

I must admit that I caught the fever and got downright aggressive myself! I was not going to walk away from my first

Mardi Gras parade empty-handed! But, you know, you feel a little silly once you get home and spread your loot on the floor. I held up the gaudy plastic beads and the cheap coins and said, "I shoved people out of the way for *this*?"

We ministers watch as the bright parade marches by us and trinkets are thrown into the crowd—salary . . . prestige . . . fame. What church leader has not felt the urge to shove forward and yell, "Throw me something, mister!" Instead of grasping for the world's dented doubloons, our desire should be to conclude our ministries holding a prize higher and holier. The apostle Peter called it the "crown of glory that will never fade away."[8]

Purifying Our Desires

As you activate your imagination in the context of prayer, then, God may replace your desires. On the other hand, He may *purify* the motives *while leaving the desires intact*. Sometimes our earthly aspirations are accurate indicators of what God wants us to do with our lives. In prayer, lay out your dream to be in demand as a speaker at student conferences. Set forth your desire to lead a large choir and orchestra. Confess your ambition to be a best-selling author. Lay out your aspirations before the the gaze of God and relinquish control over them. If God uncovers some impurity—a self-centered drive for personal adoration, for example—like a laser, God's gaze can burn that tumor off your soul while leaving the desire intact. Gone is the lust for personal acclaim; what remains is the drive to achieve great things for the glory of God and for the benefit of His church.

I am amazed at how many people misunderstand humility! They think, "If I shouldn't seek the glare of public attention, then I'll seek the shadows of obscurity. If I shouldn't promote myself, I'll belittle myself. If I shouldn't think much of myself, I'll think little of myself." Did you notice something as you read those comments, though? A minister who "nobly" says any of those statements still has the focus on himself! He's like the Amish man who left church services one Sunday and, on the buggy drive home, turned to his wife with a smile of satisfaction and said, "Wife, I do believe we were the plainest-dressed family in attendance today." He was proud of being humble! Samuel Taylor Coleridge was right. There is no greater spectacle than a prideful man aping humility.

Humility is not the state of thinking little of yourself. Humility is the state of not thinking of *yourself* at all! Humble ministers are oblivious to whether their labors bring them public acclaim or obsurity. They have a single-minded passion for God's glory and the church's benefit.

A personal checkup must be done in the context of prayer where we roll our plans upon God and abandon control of them. At the throne, God will either purify or replace our plans to bring them into line with His desires.

PERSONAL GIFTS

There is a third feature to healthy examination. Focus on your personal gifts. That sentence has two points of emphasis—focus on what *you* do well and focus on what you do *well*.

What *You* Do Well

Comparisons to others will not make for healthy self-examination. Counselor Alan McGinnis said, "Probably no habit chips away at our self-confidence quite so effectively as that of scanning the people around us to see how we compare."[9] When the Hasidic rabbi Zusya lay dying, he was asked what he thought heaven would be like. Zusya replied, "I don't know. But one thing I *do* know. When I am examined by the Lord, He will not be disappointed to find that I was not Moses or Elijah or David. I am only going to be asked, 'Why weren't you Zusya? Why weren't you fully you?'"

Praise God, our place in heaven is secure if we have been redeemed by the sacrifice of Christ. Believers will still face Christ's penetrating appraisal, though, to see whether we have built anything of value upon the foundation of salvation Christ laid. Comparing our good works to construction materials, the apostle Paul said that the returning Lord will inspect our work to see whether we built with gold, silver, and costly stones, or with the disappointing materials of wood, hay, and straw.[10] In that appraisal, we will not be compared to others. Instead we will be asked, "Why were you not everything I intended you to be?"

I am always encouraged by the two-talent servant in Jesus' parable of the talents.[11] As the story goes, a wealthy man went on a long journey. Before he went, he called three of his servants together and gave them talents—an old Greek word for large sums of money.

To one servant he gave five talents, to one he gave two, and to another servant he gave just one talent. While the master was away, the five-talent man invested the money and doubled it, as did the two-talent man. In laziness, the one-talent man buried his share of the money in a hole. On the master's return, the accounts were inspected. The master smiled at the first two and said, "Well done," while he cast the last one out of his presence.

At a surface reading, one may wonder why the two-talent man is even mentioned. I mean, the point Jesus is making is that we are to use whatever He has given us to advance the interests of God. To get that point across, all He needed was a man who used his talents and a man who failed to use his talents.

Jesus added the two-talent servant to the story to show that God assesses our work against what He gave us to do, not against what He gave *others* to do. Sure, in the parable the five-talent man brought back ten talents, while the two-talent man returned only four. Still, the point is that they both invested all they were given to advance their master's interests.

Some of us are two-talent servants. Be assured that the returning Lord will not look on us and say, "Why weren't you more like that five-talent minister? Why have you brought Me only four talents when he brought Me ten?" God assesses our work against what He gave us to do, not against what He gave others to do.

What You Do *Well*

As you resist comparisons to others and concentrate on what Christ intends *you* to be, give attention to the things you do *well*. Kennon Callahan's advice for church planning applies to a church leader's personal planning. He urged churches to plan based on strengths, not weaknesses. He said that accenting strengths is a way of acknowledging and glorifying God: "To claim them is to claim the compelling presence of God's power." Therefore, it is important to begin planning by building upon those areas where God is already at work. Callahan compared the church to a professional football team. A winning football team "runs to its strengths." If it has an all-pro right guard, right tackle, right end, and right halfback, the coach will run many plays to the right. Too many churches, however, "run to their weaknesses." In their evaluation and planning, they focus on their problems.[12]

Maybe that is what some of us do with our efforts at self-improvement. Our efforts begin with what we are *not* doing, where we are *not* effective, and what tasks we have *not* developed. Instead, we need to claim the gifts, interests, talents, and strengths God has given us. We need to give primary attention to those areas where we have allowed God to use us.

James Gunn also advises ministers to begin planning for improvement at the point of their strengths. "It is self-defeating," he writes, "to set professional goals that have no relation to what one does well and enjoys doing, and it is obvious that any evaluation of such goals would be a form of self-punishment."[13]

Of course, we should not completely dismiss our weaknesses as we evaluate our ministries. Consider again Callahan's illustration of the coach with an all-pro right guard, right tackle, right end, and right halfback. Certainly in the current season the fans would want the coach to run plays to the right. However, the fans—and the owner!—would expect the coach to be developing the left side of his line, also. He who has ears to hear, let him hear! Address your weaknesses, especially if your shortcomings are hurting yourself, your relationships, or the effectiveness of the programs you lead.

It is important, though, that you do not brood over your imperfections and end up mired in self-pity. To give primary attention to your strengths is a way of glorifying God and acknowledging His activity in your life. From such acknowledgment comes the confidence for attending to your deficiencies. Fred McGehee captures in a pithy proverb the balance we need to give in assessing our strengths and weaknesses. The career assessment consultant often advises ministers, "Make the most of your best and get some good from the rest."[14]

THE EVALUATIONS OF OTHERS

Elicit feedback on your performance as a church leader. Seek the guidance of your supervisor on staff, get comments from friends who serve in similar positions in other churches, or let a selected group of church laypersons evaluate you. Receiving comments from persons whom you serve will confirm strengths you are too shy to claim and will reveal weaknesses you are too proud to recognize. Consultants offer the following advice on evaluations.

First, choose your own advisers. Some churches have the staff supervisors, personnel committee, deacon body, or board of elders conduct annual performance reviews. You may find this formal process helpful; others, however, hesitate to be honest with areas needing work when the review is tied to one's salary!

Now, formal evaluations should not be overlooked as you develop self-improvement goals. Disregarding a formal review from those you serve would be both pragmatically foolish and spiritually arrogant. In Proverbs we are told, "He who is often reproved, yet stiffens his neck will suddenly be broken beyond healing."[15] Over the years of directing the work of others, I have seen this proverb tragically played out in the lives of a few.

When it comes to the freedom to confess weaknesses to others—and when it comes to being receptive to the criticism of others—no formal process a church devises can substitute for the evaluations of those whom you have handpicked.

Personal growth is most likely to take place when you make yourself accountable to a group that you have selected for their ability to be both honest and encouraging with you. As one pastor put it, "*Asking* for a critique [as opposed to submitting to a formal review] transforms the environment. . . . Instead of being cast in the role of an employee wondering if the bosses are happy, I'm put in the position of a leader soliciting candid advice."[16]

Second, performance reviews should be limited to your objectives, your goals, and your efforts at fulfilling them. Why waste time with evaluations over items that both you and the church have agreed are unimportant to your work? With the help of your chosen group, prepare a simple survey sheet. Make sure you have a combination of quantitative and qualitative responses. The following is an example of a quantitative response based on one of my objectives:

Objective 4: "I will train and motivate God's people to do the work of ministry." *Overall, I have been (check one):*

____5. Very effective in meeting this objective

____4. Effective

____3. Somewhat effective

____2. Below average

____1. Ineffective

The reviewer simply places a check mark by the most appropriate response. Quantitative responses are easy not only for the reviewer to use but also for the minister to grade. The minister can determine his overall "score" by averaging the numerical ratings returned by the evaluators.

Notice, too, the careful wording to which the reviewers must respond. Experts have found that reviewers are more comfortable responding to the words "very effective," "effective," and "ineffective," instead of "excellent," "average," and "poor."

Apparently, reviewers consider being asked to evaluate a person's "effectiveness" focuses on performance while being asked to evaluate a person's "excellence" focuses on character. Since your reviewers will be more comfortable evaluating your *performance*, they will more likely provide honest responses.

In addition, evaluation forms should provide evaluators an opportunity to state opinions in their own words. The following statements are examples of qualitative review:

If I could do last year's ministry over, what, if anything, should I change?

_____

_____

_____

_____

Please tell me the top three ways my ministry helped you last year.

_____

_____

_____

_____

If you are a volunteer worker under my leadership, tell me what ways, if any, I could be more effective in leading the workers.

_____

_____

_____

_____

In this format, the reviewer is asked to state his opinion in his own words. Notice the little phrase "if anything" or "if any" in two of the above statements. Experts have found without it some people will feel obligated to answer your question, even if they have no strong opinion on the issue. Give them an opportunity to leave the question blank by adding the little phrase, "if anything."

Third, in most cases the chosen reviewers should complete the survey forms and then share their answers orally with the person being reviewed. Although at times a minister needs to solicit anonymous comments from the church at large, the most helpful reviews will be from those whom the minister has personally selected. They should first write their answers on the evaluation form, and then share their answers orally with the minister either one-on-one or in a group with the other reviewers.

Writing the review first allows the adviser to organize his thoughts and provide more meaningful comments. Also, when he shares the review with you verbally, you can ask for clarification of unclear comments. Though you may believe that anonymous reviews make for honest reviews, sometimes unsigned surveys can be unclear at best and unfair at worst.

THE EMPHASES OF YOUR CHURCH
AND THE LARGER CHRISTIAN FELLOWSHIP

As you reflect on how your service measures up to your manifesto, give attention to your church and its local, state, and national memberships. Also, ask yourself how God could use you in the larger Christian fellowship beyond the borders of your denomination. Think about how these communities of faith could both receive help from you and give help to you.

Receiving Help from You

What does your local church most need of you now? God has called you to be not simply a minister, but a minister to a specific congregation at a specific point in that congregation's history. A large suburban congregation meeting in a new worship center may need a music minister to develop a polished, professional worship service. A congregation in a transitional neighborhood may need a pastor to help them negotiate a transfer of the property to an ethnic mission. A church reeling from controversy with its former minister to students may need nothing more than a demonstration of character, stability, and patience from its new youth pastor.

While considering your church's needs, don't forget your denomination. Consider all three levels—local, state, and national. Are there positions, projects, and priorities of the denomination that could use your help?

You may be given the privilege of serving on denominational committees or boards. Perhaps your local association could use your training as a student minister in starting a new Bible study on a college campus. Maybe you have a language or a skill that would be helpful in leading a short-term project in the foreign missions field. Evaluate what such opportunities would require from you. You may be given opportunities to expand your kingdom service beyond the local church and the denominational structure. A friend of mine led his church to write an AIDS policy so that the congregation would have some guidelines for informed service to those who are HIV-positive. As a result, numerous churches have asked him to conduct seminars to help them write an AIDS policy, and he completed a doctor of ministry project on the subject. I imagine he will write a book soon. Within the congregation he serves as pastor, and among the larger Christian fellowship, he is fulfilling the ministerial objective of equipping the saints for the work of ministry.

Giving Help to You

Our churches are rich with human resources to help us improve ourselves as ministers. In my last congregation, God brought to our fellowship not one, but two management consultants who operated their own firms. The conversation and materials they provided helped me immeasurably as an administrator.

We ministers have coaches in our congregations who may be willing to help us improve our physical fitness. We have English teachers who may be willing to help us improve our public speaking. We have professional counselors who may be willing to help us develop our counseling skills or who may even take us on as clients in our efforts to develop better relationships with our mates, our children, and our co-workers. Since "God has arranged the parts in the body, every one of them, just as he wanted them to be," [17] consider the human resources He has placed in the fellowship you serve—resources that can help you improve yourself.

In addition, denominational offices and interdenominational ministries offer services to help you become a better minister. Perhaps this year your state convention's Church-Minister Relations division is hosting a seminar on time management for ministers. Maybe an agency of the national convention has a special workshop on recruiting and leading volunteers—something you identify as a weak spot in your ministry. Again, an interdenominational ministry such as the Willow Creek Community Church might offer a workshop on directing dramatic sketches for worship services. In your personal checkup, evaluate how the larger Christian fellowship might help you become a better minister.

SOCIAL FACTORS

Finally, identify social factors that might give you clues to what God wants from you at this point in your life. What does your community most need of you right now?

During the years I served a church in the capital city of Baton Rouge, my community most needed a pro-life message that was both reasonable and urgent. During debate over a law that would have given the state of Louisiana responsibility to provide justice for preborn little ones, I became convinced that there was a divine reason I was pastoring in the city where the legislature convened. The social setting gave me clues to what I believed

God wanted from me at that point in my ministry. So, I prepared myself to speak on this issue and was given an opportunity to address the committees of both houses of the state legislature.

Of course, not all of our community involvement will be so public. Most of our work at being salt and light will be out of the headlines. God placed you in your field of service for a reason. What clues can you pick up from the neighborhood that help you decide what God wants from you? What community concerns demand your leadership: illiteracy, unemployment, chemical dependency, teen promiscuity and pregnancy, hunger and homelessness, domestic violence?

"The place God calls you," wrote Frederick Buechner, "is the place where your deep gladness and the world's deep hunger meet."[18] That combination of personal fulfillment and social need will compel a college minister to lead her students on a summer mission trip to repair homes for the poor. It will convince a white pastor that he needs to learn conversational Spanish to minister effectively to the large Hispanic population in his neighborhood. It will cause music ministers to bring their choirs together, the one from a predominately white church and the other from a predominately black church, for a music festival on Race Relations Sunday in February.

EXAMINE YOURSELF

Hold your manifesto in one hand and your mirror in the other. Are you the kind of minister that God expects you to be in your unique field and with your one-of-a-kind mix of education, experience, and interests? Dream about the ways you would like to be used of God. Through prayer, give your plans to God and relinquish control of them. Inventory the ways God has used you and thank God for those strengths. Use survey forms to discover the strengths and weaknesses that others identify in you. Reflect on what God might expect of you in your church, denomination, and the larger Christian community. Examine the gnawing needs of the neighborhood for clues of what God expects of you.

Once you have examined your current ministry, you must set some goals for personal improvement. That third step toward being an intentional minister will be the focus of our next chapter. Before continuing, however, take a moment to complete the following activity.

ACTIVITY

Plan an escape to a quiet place for an hour or two. You will need some uninterrupted time for this exercise. Make about 10-15 copies of the next page, labeled "Personal Checkup." Take one copy and write your first objective from your manifesto. Use the questions on the Personal Checkup and reflect on where you are and where you want to be regarding that first objective. Do the same with the other objectives.

PERSONAL CHECKUP

Objective:

_____

_____

_____

Imagination (Some things I'd like to accomplish under this objective):

_____

_____

_____

Prayer (Reflections after praying about this objective):

_____

_____

_____

Strengths (Things I do well in fulfillment of this objective):

_____

_____

_____

Weaknesses (Things that need my attention as I think about this objective):

_____

_____

Church, Denomination, Christian Community (How my church, denomination, and the larger Christian community could use my help or give me help regarding this objective):

_____

_____

Neighborhood (Social issues that might be clues to what God wants me doing in my community):

_____

_____

F O U R

THE THIRD STEP: SET GOALS FOR PERSONAL IMPROVEMENT

If your heart be not set on the end of your labors . . . you
are not likely to see much fruit of it. . . . I have observed
that God seldom blesses any man's work so much as his
whose heart is set upon success.

— Richard Baxter (1615–91)

E D KOCH HAD AN UNUSUAL WAY of greeting
people. Instead of a "How are you doing?" the flamboy-
ant former mayor of New York City would extend his
hand with a "Hi! How am I doing?" He wanted to know what
people thought of his leadership.

We know what it means to greet peers with a cheery "How's
your ministry going?" but inside we are really asking, "How is
my ministry doing?" Each of us has had our seasons of comparing our activities to the activities of others, our buildings to the
buildings of others, the attendance at our events to the attendance at another minister's events. In such comparisons, we have
hoped to find our labors progressing toward anything we could
call "solid achievement."

An intentional minister, though, is free from fretting over
whether his or her ministry is having any progress. By writing

75

out goals, he has defined what progress means to him. And by monitoring his pursuit of the goals, he can determine whether he is making progress. After writing a ministry manifesto and using it for personal evaluation, we need to take the third step toward being intentional ministers. We need to prepare goals from the raw material of our self-evaluation.

GETTING PERSONAL

Have you heard the one about the seminary professor whose favorite subject was the topic of Christian love? He would harp on the subject in his seminary classes. He would address it in his sermons when he was invited to preach. He even lectured his kids about the importance of love whenever he caught them arguing.

One day he was pouring a new walkway for his front yard. Just when he had put the final touches on his work and the cement was beginning to harden, a football hit the wet cement with a thud. Three neighborhood boys sloshed in to pick up their ball. Red with anger, the professor slammed down his trowel, came up to the boys with his arms flailing, and gave them a tongue-lashing over their stupidity.

After the boys cowered away, the professor's wife stepped outside the house and said, "Honey, for someone who's always telling people to love each other, that wasn't very loving." The professor replied, "Dear, I love those boys in the abstract, but not in the concrete!" (Okay, you're groaning now, but you'll tell it to the next person you see, won't you?)

When we set a goal from the raw material of our self-evaluation, we are moving from the abstract to the concrete. Our manifestos declare what we believe any minister in any setting should do. Our goals declare what actions we will complete in our specific setting to be that kind of minister.

For example, an associate pastor may have the following objective: "I will equip the deacons to be effective in the work of pastoral ministry." Moving from the abstract to the concrete, the minister might make the following goal to fulfill such an objective: "For the next six months, I will take a deacon with me on every hospital visit I make and review the visit with him afterward."

Again, a youth pastor might have an objective to "set an example of discipleship for the students I serve." After a moment of self-evaluation, he finds that he misses the benefits of the Scripture memorization plan he used years ago in college. He commits to "challenge the students to join me in memorizing a Scripture verse from the Sunday School lesson each week during the next year."

Notice the way these ministers moved from abstractions about what church leaders *should* be to plans for what kind of church leaders they *will* be.

Admittedly, goals sound less lofty than objectives. After stating my grand objective to be an accurate and relevant communicator of God's Word, it surely sounds mundane to set a goal of meeting once a quarter with a selected group of church members who will review my sermon delivery. But without such tangible commitments, our ideals remain pipe dreams. An intentional minister makes sure he puts his self-improvement plans in concrete.

WHY SET GOALS?

Management specialist Tom McConalogue reported the results of a survey of eighty managers regarding goals. While over 90 percent agreed with the statement that establishing goals was "a cornerstone of effective management," less than 40 percent regretfully admitted that they had no goals.[1] I imagine he would have found the same results had he surveyed ministers. We all pay lip service to the importance of goals even when we never set any. He concluded that leaders, and those who train them, should put more emphasis on the initiating dimension of leadership.

Even if leaders are lax in *setting* goals, we readily admit *needing* goals. Why? Above any other reason, goals describe in bold, vivid terms the future we believe God wants for us and for those our lives touch. A goal, then, is a statement of faith. Ed Dayton points out:

> If we refuse to make any statements about the future, if we shy away from describing the kind of world we believe God desires, or the kind of relationships he wants us to have, then we have no real commitment to the Kingdom. Vague feelings about what might be best are substituted for real commitment.[2]

The highest and holiest reason to set written commitments for our work, then, is to present tangible offerings before the Lord. Beyond that, there are secondary reasons to have goals. Our written commitments impact our relationships with our peers, our effectiveness, our sense of fulfillment, and even our physical health.

Free to Enjoy the Ministry of Others

While ministers have been forced to leave churches for breaking the Seventh Commandment of the Decalogue, as far as I know no minister has been terminated for violating the Tenth Commandment. Nevertheless, God expects us to live above coveting, just as He expects us to live above adultery. The envious resentment against another minister's opportunities or accomplishments should have no place in the life of God's servants.

In John 21, Simon Peter illustrates how easy it is to get our attention off our own divine assignments and focus on our peers. Simon Peter had nearly lost his apostleship over denying his relationship with Jesus. Following the resurrection, Jesus re-instated the big fisherman to the apostolate. Jesus said to him, "Feed my sheep" and "Follow me." But no sooner had Jesus given Peter his mission than the impetuous apostle turned his attention on a peer. "Lord," he said, pointing to another disciple (probably John), "what about him?" Jesus replied, "What is it to you? You follow me."

Since goal-setting springs out of a desire to be all God wants *us* to be, the process can protect us from comparing and coveting. We will focus our attention only on our own stewardship. And when we are free from jealous comparisons, we are free to give attention to the hurts of other ministers and to enjoy the contributions of other ministers.

I imagine many of us could agree with the frustration of Robert Jeffress, pastor of the First Baptist Church in Wichita Falls, Texas. He wrote:

> Every year I travel to our denomination's annual convention and return with a resolve never to go again. I am constantly encountering egotistical preachers who are trying to climb over one another on their way up the success ladder. I think of one in particular. This pastor is consumed with the desire to be number one. He is interested in you only if you can help him achieve his goal. When you talk with him, he will never look you in the eye. Instead, his eyes are constantly darting around the room seemingly checking to see if there is anyone more important than you with whom he should be conversing.[3]

Only when we get ourselves off our hands can we develop genuine friendships with our peers in the ministry. And our fellow servants desperately need genuine friendships. This job exerts profound pressure on our families; it takes its toll on our physical well-being. Criticism, while at times offered kindly by people with a sincere desire to help, is too often offered rudely by self-appointed guardians of the church's best interests. Natural tensions occasionally arise between even the best workers in the programs we lead. The counseling and crisis visitation drain our emotional reservoirs.

Thank God for the church members who offer words of encouragement and the promise of prayers. But nothing can substitute for the support of a peer who knows the unique demands of this calling! Giving attention to our own goals sets us free to enjoy the successes and bear the burdens of our fellow servants.

A Focus for the Use of Our Resources

Goal-setting keeps us from wasting the precious resources God has invested in us—our time, our talents, our income, and our energy. Without a defined direction for the use of our resources, our ministries end up looking like the scattered, indiscriminate spray of a shotgun blast! That's the way James Gaines described his work before God impressed him with the need for an intentional ministry. Gaines wrote:

> In the early days of my professional ministry pilgrimage, I adopted the shotgun method. I had an abundance of energy and found myself scurrying all over the place trying to get everything done; and in these bursts of energy, I hoped to find personal and professional fulfillment. Needless to say, all I found was that at the end of the day I was tired physically, emotionally, intellectually, and spiritually. But even more debilitating was the keen feeling of frustration and confusion that seemed to overwhelm my ministry. . . . At this juncture God led me to understand the importance of planning and setting professional as well as individual ministry goals.[4]

We need to learn in our labors what civil engineers have learned in nature. Engineers know that if they dam up a river and channel the water into a narrow passage, the mighty force of that focused water can drive turbines fast enough to generate electricity. In fact, a third of the world's electricity is produced in these hydroelectric plants. There is a power in focused water. We need to translate that lesson into our efforts at effective ministry: There is a power in focused activity. As we quit dissipating our time, talents, income, and energy and instead channel them into fulfilling well-defined goals, we find that the process generates useful power.

A Sense of Accomplishment

Students of human behavior have confirmed that people need a sense of progress or achievement to consider their work and lives meaningful. Eugene Heimler, a Holocaust survivor, wrote of a Nazi experiment in meaningless labor. Jews were moved from a prison factory, where the work had been hard but purposeful, to the out-of-doors where they were ordered to move sand from one end of their camp to another. They carted sand to one end of the labor camp and then reloaded and carted it back to the other end—day after day, week after week, month after month. Many prisoners lost their minds and were shot by the guards. Others threw themselves into the electrified fence. Heimler recalled the commandant remarking one day that "now there is no need to use the crematoria."[5]

Human beings need some sense of purpose to their labors. Yet those of us who work with souls receive so little assured results from our labors. I mean, how often can we point to tangible results from our work? We cannot measure what effect our sermons or our choir anthems had on the congregation last week. We have no way of knowing what part our counseling played in someone's recovery.

There have been times I long for the "good old days" when I worked on a dynamite crew. During a summer break from the university, I went to work for a road construction company. I was assigned to help a man blast rock in a quarry. We would drill deep holes, plug sticks of dynamite with electric charges, wire the charges together, and place the sticks in the holes. Then, for the last act of the day, we would clear the area and set off the explosion. The ground shook from the blast, shook again as the boulders tumbled back to earth, and our day was over. Without a doubt, I went home from that job with a sense of completion. I've rarely been able to see such dramatic results from the work I do as a pastor!

Still, that need for a sense of accomplishment will come out in one way or another. Perhaps that is why some of us rattle off a long inventory of buildings constructed, renovations completed, and numbers enrolled when asked how our ministries have been going. We need some tangible assessment of our work. Half-joking and half-serious, one minister admitted:

> In every church where I have been, I have left behind an astonishing array of electrical connections. It finally came to me that the reason I periodically get an irresistible urge to crawl under the church floor or fish wires through conduits is that, when the job is done, and I push a button—something happens.[6]

Meaningful goal-setting can provide the sense of progress and achievement that is often so elusive for ministers.

A Contribution to Health

I was surprised to read that medication for stress-related illnesses ranked second only to maternity expenses in the Southern Baptist Convention's medical plan.[7] In fact, studies from numerous denominations conclude that those in church vocations are under intense pressure.

Now for the good news. Some recent studies suggest that goal-setting can contribute to our physical health. It stands to reason that we reduce both mental anxiety and physical tension when we base our actions on what we want to accomplish. A recent book, *Getting Well Again*, even makes a case for pursuing goals as an effective strategy against cancer.[8] Hope contributes to health, and goals are codified hopes.

THE TEN COMMANDMENTS
OF GOOD GOAL-SETTING

Considering such benefits of written commitments, goal-setting should become second nature for a leader. As you set goals for the improvement of your ministry, keep in mind ten criteria for good goals.

The First Commandment: Thou Shalt Have Written Goals

"I know my goals," one minister told me, "but I keep them in my head. I don't need to write them down." Christian businessman Fred Smith remembers the time he tried that excuse when working for Maxey Jarman. "I know my goal, but I can't put it in words," he told his boss. Jarman replied, "The only reason you can't write it is because you don't know it. When you know it, you can write it." Throughout the years, Smith found that writing his goals "knocked the fuzz" off his thinking.[9] Nothing is properly defined until you write it down. In addition, management consultants contend that when goals are written, not only do the goals become more specific, but the probability of achieving them increases.

The probability increased for Curtis Carlson, and with dramatic results. When Carlson was twenty-four, he founded the Gold Bond Stamp Company. Even though the nation was in the middle of the Great Depression, Carlson set a goal of earning a princely one hundred dollars a week. He wrote down that aim and carried the slip of paper in his pocket until the edges were frayed. Today Carlson Companies, Inc. has annual revenues of over 9 billion dollars. Carlson believes in written goals. "Writing out a goal crystallizes it in my mind," says Carlson. "I can quickly evaluate whether decisions will take me toward that [goal] or away from it."[10] Imagine how effective we could be for the kingdom if we had goals written on frayed slips of paper that we could pull from our pockets and review from time to time!

The Second Commandment: Thou Shalt Put a Deadline on Every Goal

Goals without deadlines quickly become daydreams. But a limit on a goal's lifespan gives us the urgency we need to accomplish it.

Even if you are setting a goal for starting a behavior that should never end, at least set a date at which you will pause and measure your progress. For example, you might set a goal to jump-start a stalled devotional life. You would hope that, once you returned to a plan of daily Bible reading, you would stick to it throughout your life. Still, set a goal to stay on the reading schedule for one quarter. At that juncture you can review your progress and decide whether to change the goal or extend the deadline. You will more likely stick to your goal if you set a date at which you plan to stop and review your progress. If you find the goal manageable after one quarter (or whatever period you set), you can easily extend the deadline. Over time, the habit should become so much a part of your life that you will not need to make yourself accountable to a goal.

The Third Commandment: Thou Shalt Set Measurable Goals

The statement, "I will be more evangelistic," is a wish, not a goal. As a result, you will have to evaluate the achievement of this wish by nothing but moods and impressions. If you *feel* more evangelistic over time, then you will mentally reward yourself. On the other hand, if you *feel* that you still cannot describe yourself as an evangelistic minister, you will mentally lash yourself.

Instead, why not decide ahead of time just how you plan to evaluate yourself? Then focus your efforts on measuring up to that predetermined evaluation. For example, "In the next year I will share the plan of salvation with at least one person each week." One can measure the achievement of such a goal. If you fail to invite fifty-two persons to receive the gift of eternal life next year, you have failed to achieve the goal. In addition, it is easy to see that by pursuing such a measurable goal you are more likely to be more evangelistic than by pursuing the lofty but unreckonable wish to "be more evangelistic."

I remember what an old farmer told me in the rural church I served while a student at the university. He said, "Son, wish in one hand and spit in the other and see which one fills up faster."

No doubt a graphic way to discover what wishing will get you—nothing! Intentional ministers track their progress with *measurable* goals.

The Fourth Commandment: Thou Shalt Set Goals That Are Challenging, but Attainable

Make sure your goals are challenging enough to liberate you from the island of Lilliput! In the 1700s, Jonathan Swift wrote a biting satire about the travels of a fictional ship's surgeon named Lemuel Gulliver. During the first part of *Gulliver's Travels,* the doctor becomes stranded on the island of Lilliput—a land of people one-twelfth the size of normal people. The Lilliputians treat Gulliver well at first and, in turn, the doctor helps them. In time, though, the tiny people turn against him and Gulliver is glad to escape from the little people. We can keep from being annoyed by Lilliputian pursuits if we will define what well-done ministry means to us and then pursue challenging goals based on that definition.

The fine art of goal-setting requires an aim that is challenging without being unattainable. Make sure that what you have committed to do is within your reach. I remember a sales trainer who disagreed with me on this point. As I shared this principle of goal-setting with my church, he said, "No, no. You should set aggressive goals." I agreed that goals should be challenging, but then he went on to explain his definition of "aggressive" goals: "If you can reach your goals, it's because you set them too low." I privately felt sorry for his sales team!

Some people, like this trainer, believe that setting impossibly high goals can be a catalyst for motivation. The opposite actually results. Goals set too high get abandoned. Grandiose goals fail to motivate us for at least two reasons. First, they make us discouraged when it becomes obvious we will never reach them. And second, we never even start to work on the goals because we fail to take them to heart as genuine possibilities for our self-improvement.

Goal-setting is more art than science. What is a ridiculous target for you at this point in your ministry may be a very reasonable target later. And what is attainable for one minister may be impossible for another. Consider an associate pastor who is divinely convicted about his poor attention to personal contacts with prospective and new church members. Zealously, he sets a goal to reverse years of poor practice by making five hundred in-home visits per year, or roughly ten a week. Most likely, he should begin with a more reasonable goal, for example, three to seven contacts, and then work up to a more aggressive policy.

On the other hand, when I introduced the concepts in this book to a friend of mine, he set a goal to memorize all sixty of the cards found at the end of the second chapter within eighteen months. Knowing my friend, the goal was not unreachable. For years, he has been in the habit of memorizing portions of Scripture, and he knows his capabilities.

Admittedly, there is difficulty in determining how high is too high for the Christian. Nothing is impossible with God. Hebrews 11:1 tells us that it is the very nature of faith to be sure of what we hope for and to be certain of what we do not see. The writer goes on to list off those who overcame impossible odds because God had called them to some duty. The craft of goal-setting requires us to determine when our goals come from a divine calling and when they come from our own empty boastings. The first kind of goal is properly challenging while the second kind is just presumptuous. Fine-tune your goal-setting process until you are making commitments that are neither ridiculously low nor impossibly high.

The Fifth Commandment: Thou Shalt Limit Goals to Outcomes You Can Control

Lyle Schaller said, "Perhaps the most common pitfall in the goal-setting process is the temptation to set goals in areas over which those setting the goals do not have control."[11] For example, a minister of education has no control over how many Sunday School teachers actually contact their absentees before the next class. She does have control over how often and how well she impresses upon them the importance of making contacts to absent members. And, of course, there is often a connection between the two.

A poor goal, then, would be "to have 90 percent of my workers make weekly contacts with their absent members." This minister would have better control over one of the following goals. She could set a goal to "set aside time in the annual worker's retreat to address the reasons my teachers do not contact absentees based on a survey of those reasons." She could commit to "find a teacher who regularly contacts his absentees and enlist him for the annual worker's retreat to share some personal anecdotes that illustrate the benefits of weekly contacts." She could determine that she would "create a program that would publicly recognize workers who contact four absentees a month." Any one of these goals would more likely achieve the desired end of increasing absentee contacts than a goal to "have 90 percent of my workers make weekly contacts with their absent members."

The Sixth Commandment: Thou Shalt Make Goals in Keeping with Stated Objectives

If you cannot justify a goal under one of your stated objectives, one of two things must take place. On the one hand, you may need to abandon the goal. By comparing a goal to his ministry manifesto, a church leader sometimes discovers that the activity will not contribute to his vision of the ideal minister. And why be distracted from that vision by irrelevant pursuits?

On the other hand, if a goal cannot fit into the ministry manifesto you prepared at the end of the second chapter, you may need to rewrite your objectives. In the process of self-evaluation and goal-setting, a church leader sometimes finds that he defined his ministry manifesto too narrowly. He finds that he must return to Step One and rephrase his objectives in such a way that they include all that he believes Christ has called him to be.

The Seventh Commandment: Thou Shalt Not Let Goals Conflict with Other Goals

Our self-evaluation will uncover some areas in which we want to improve and naturally we will want to start to work in all of these areas immediately. As a result, we will be tempted to assign ourselves projects that begin right away and end all at the same time. If we give in to that naive eagerness, though, our schedules will become too hectic and we will abandon our self-improvement plans.

Instead, spread your goals across the months of the calendar. Stagger the start and stop dates. Make sure there will be no conflict between the actions required to achieve the various goals (to be discussed in chap. 5). Just as you should be mindful not to set impossibly high goals, be mindful not to dissipate your energy into too many goals at one time.

The Eighth Commandment: Thou Shalt Be Specific, Not Vague

A goal to "develop my spiritual life" is too vague. A better goal in this vein would be, "I will read six devotional classics by this time next year." Or, "In the next year, I will set aside the first fifteen minutes of every office day to pray and read Scripture." Or, "I will complete the course *Experiencing God*[12] over the summer" (a worthy and life-changing goal, I might add!).

When writing your goals, be concrete. Avoid describing your goals with words like *approximate, as soon as possible, maximum, minimum, satisfactory, reasonable,* and *adequate.* Instead, go ahead and define what results would be "reasonable," and when "as soon as possible" would fall on the calendar. Stay away from verbs like *know, understand, appreciate,* and *enjoy.* Use action verbs—*write, list, assign, design, point to.*

I like Robert Mager's way of ensuring that one has worded a goal specifically. He suggests that the "Hey, Dad" test be used on every goal. Mager writes:

> You simply use the substance of the statement to finish the sentence: Hey, Dad, let me show you how I can _____! If the result is absurd and makes you want to laugh, you are dealing with a statement broad enough to be considered an abstraction rather than a performance. For example: Hey, Dad, let me show you how I can internalize my growing awareness! (Yeah? Lemme see you!).[13]

Since a minister's goals are ultimately offerings before our Heavenly Father, the "Hey, Dad" test takes on a unique meaning for us! Perhaps we would improve both the preparation and pursuit of our goals if we began each goal with, "Heavenly Father, let me show You how I can _____!"

The Ninth Commandment: Thou Shalt Specify a Single Key Result to Be Accomplished, Not Two or Three

Of course, there may be several steps implied in the pursuit of the goal, but the goal itself must have a single key result to be accomplished. The following goal a minister of childhood education might set should really be broken into two goals: "By this time next year I will make one visit to each of my volunteer workers and have three workers evaluate my leadership." The first half of the goal appears to be designed to help the minister become better acquainted with his team, while the second half of the goal seems to be motivated by a desire to improve his working style. Both concerns are important, but they do not belong in the same goal statement. A good goal delineates only one key result to be accomplished.

The Tenth Commandment: Thou Shalt Limit Goals to "What" and "When," and Not Answer "How" and "Why"

As you write your goals, certain questions will come to mind—How will I achieve this goal? What steps must I take and in what order should I take them? Will I need to purchase anything to complete this goal and, if so, how much will it cost? Is there anyone who could help me perform this goal? All of these questions are important, but these issues will be addressed in your action plan (which will be discussed in chap. 5).

Your goal statement does not need to explain "how" you plan to achieve the goal. Neither do you have to explain "why" you should go after the goal. That question was answered in the objective. In the goal itself, you are stating simply what measurable result must take place by a certain deadline.

BE A GOAL-GETTER!

An intentional minister does not leave his desire for self-improvement in the abstract. He puts his dreams in concrete by designing well-written goals. His goals state in bold and accurate terms the future he believes God wants for him and for those his ministry touches. Use the following activity to make goals out of the raw material of the self-evaluation you performed at the end of chapter 3.

ACTIVITY

At the end of chapter 3, you were encouraged to evaluate your ministry against your objectives. No doubt you found several areas in which you wanted improvement under each objective. But in this activity, you are asked to set only one goal under each of your objectives.

There is no "magic formula" to setting only one goal per objective. You are being asked to limit your goals only for the purpose of this exercise. Through the practice of goal-setting, intentional ministers discover how many goals they can reasonably pursue at once.

After you have a set of goals that reflect a genuine commitment to improve yourself, examine the goals in light of the ten commandments of good goal-setting in this chapter. Make several photocopies of the following page, entitled "Goal-Setting Checklist." Write your first goal on a copy of this checklist and answer the questions. Modify your written commitment until you are able to answer "yes" to every question. Do the same with your other goals.

GOAL-SETTING CHECKLIST

Goal:

_____

_____

_____

Adjust your goal statement until you can circle "yes" on the following questions:

Yes or No   My goal is written. (We'll start with an easy one!).

Yes or No   My goal has a deadline.

Yes or No   The results of my goal can be measured.

Yes or No   My goal is attainable, but it still challenges my limits.

Yes or No   My goal is limited to outcomes I can control.

Yes or No   My goal is in keeping with my objectives. This goal falls under the following objective:

_____

_____

Yes or No   This goal has been written with my other goals in mind to make sure they do not conflict.

Yes or No   My goal is worded specifically, not vaguely. It makes sense when I complete the following sentence with my goal: "Heavenly Father, let me show you how I can _____."

Yes or No   My goal specifies a single key result to be accomplished, not two or three.

Yes or No   My goal simply answers the questions "what will be done" and "when it will be done." My goal does not answer "why" or "how."

FIVE

THE FOURTH STEP:
SET ACTION PLANS

"Would you tell me, please, which way I ought to go from here?" asked Alice.

"That depends a great deal on where you want to go," replied the Cheshire cat.

"I don't much care where," said Alice.

"Then it doesn't matter which way you go."

— *Alice in Wonderland*

WHAT'S THE LATEST IN HIGH-TECH gadgetry? Personal navigation devices. Travelers can be guided on their way by units small enough to be held in the hand or mounted to an automobile dashboard. The *Wall Street Journal* recently reported on the businesses that are trying to bring personal navigation devices to the mass market.[1]

For example, Blaupunkt has introduced their TravelPilot, which displays on a four-and-a-half-inch screen a driver's present location and the best route to get where he wants to go. In Pinellas County, Florida, Lifefleet ambulance drivers use navigation equipment to find unfamiliar addresses in twenty-five communities. An in-car system from the Pioneer Electronic Corporation even includes data on nearby restaurants.

Of course, this new technology is still pricey. Then again, it may be well worth the money never to have to fold another road map!

Personal navigation devices may soon be as commonplace as wristwatches, helping travelers choose the best route to get to their destinations. When planning for self-improvement, we also need to determine the best routes to reach our goals. An action plan represents the route we have chosen in pursuit of a goal.

After writing his declaration of ideal ministry, examining his ministry against the mission statement, and writing goals in keeping with his manifesto, the intentional minister takes a fourth step. He maps out how he plans to reach those goals. An action plan is a series of necessary actions that the minister must take to reach his goal.

For example, consider the following goal: "During the summer I will preach a seven-week sermon series on contemporary social issues suggested by the church and the surrounding community." To begin fulfilling the goal in July, I would have to take several necessary actions. I would need to create a survey form for people to indicate what social issues they want me to address. I would have to implement two promotional campaigns—one to promote the survey forms and another to promote the sermon series once the topics have been selected. I would need to give myself time to research the topics that had been chosen. My music director would also need a list of what topic would be addressed on a given Sunday.

Looking over that random list of activities, ask yourself in what order they would need to be accomplished. Creating the survey form would have to come first, followed by a campaign to promote the use of the forms. I would have to set a deadline for the completion of the survey forms. After the deadline, I would have to tally the results and choose the seven topics, assigning each a spot on my Sunday morning preaching calendar. This would give me the material I need to perform the next step: designing and implementing a campaign to promote the seven-part series in the church and the community. My music director would need to be informed so that he could coordinate his plans with the sermon each Sunday. I would have to gather research on the topics ahead of time to avoid doing research on the same week I have to write the sermon.

What would a final action plan look like on this goal? In fact, this was a goal for my own preaching ministry some time ago. The following was my action plan:

1. By the third Thursday in May, create a survey form to distribute to the church and community. Provide possible sermon titles for twenty contemporary social issues. Instruct the respondent to choose seven. Provide blanks for the respondent to suggest other topics that I might have missed.

2. Prepare a campaign to promote the use of the survey forms. The sermon series will be called *Seven Sizzlin' Subjects*. Place a form in the community newspaper, the church newsletter, and in the bulletins every Sunday. Encourage church members to complete a form themselves, but also distribute copies of the form to their unchurched neighbors and co-workers. Run this campaign between the fourth Sunday in May and third Sunday in June. The third Sunday in June will be the deadline to return the completed forms.

3. On Monday following the deadline, tally the results of the survey forms and choose the topics, assigning them a date on my preaching calendar.

4. On Tuesday following the deadline, confer with the music director regarding the preaching calendar.

5. Prepare a campaign to promote the *Seven Sizzlin' Subjects* sermon series. Place ads in the community newspaper and the church newsletter. The promotional campaign will run from the last Sunday in June to the second Sunday in July.

6. From the last Sunday in June to the first Sunday in July, gather research on the topics.

7. The *Seven Sizzlin' Subjects* series will begin the second Sunday
    in July and run to the fourth Sunday in August.

ASKING QUESTIONS

If you followed the ten commandments of good goal-setting in
chapter 4, you have a set of goals that state only what you will
accomplish by a certain date. *Why* you should pursue the goal
is answered in your mission statement. *How* you should pursue
the goal is answered in the action plans you write following this
chapter.

Most likely, you have already begun to ask yourself the best
way to fulfill your goals. An action plan answers at least five
questions regarding how a goal should be achieved.

Question 1:

"What method or methods will I use?"

Consider the following goal that a pastor might set: "This year
I will begin a witness training course in my church." The pastor
has several methods to achieve this goal. He could design his
own course. He could choose to attend clinics offered him by
his denominational headquarters. There are a number of excellent programs available.

The action plan for this goal should include what method he
plans to use to fulfill the goal.

Again, consider a preschool minister who determines to make
a non-crisis visit with every preschool worker twice a year. She
could choose various methods to fulfill this goal. She could set
aside an hour every Sunday afternoon for visiting, she could plan
to meet a different worker for lunch every Monday, or she could
plan to set aside one Saturday afternoon a month to visit in the
homes of four workers. She will more likely achieve her goal if
she uses a written action plan to think through *how* she plans to
achieve her goal.

Have you asked yourself what processes you will use to achieve your goals? Make sure that the action plans you prepare answer the question, "What method or methods will I use to complete my commitment?"

Question 2:

"What costs are involved?"

As you prepare to work on your goal, count the costs. What materials will you have to purchase? What registration fees and travel expenses will you have to incur for conferences? What charges will you be billed if you have to hire consultants and other professionals? If you must pay the expenses out of your own pocket, see to it that your family's budget can sustain the additional burden. If the church will pick up the costs, make sure the costs will be supported in the budget your church allows you.

Question 3:

"Who will I need to enlist or consult as I pursue this goal?"

Some of our goals may require the help of others to achieve. For example, a music director who wants to learn how to use MIDI technology in his ministry may want to enlist the help of a colleague in the music department of the local college. Again, a youth minister who wants to begin a personal weight management program may want to set up an appointment with a nutritionist who attends her congregation.

Of course, you will not need the help of others to accomplish every personal goal. But there are times when you will want to consult other persons even though their help is not needed. The pursuit of some goals will affect a secretary, a marriage partner, or a peer on staff. In forming your action plan, make sure to consult those who will have to make personal adjustments to your new commitments.

For example, time away at a conference will certainly affect a marriage partner—especially if you leave your spouse to take care of children alone! A decision to complete a seminary degree will mean you will have less time available for your church. (In fact, some seminaries require you to submit a form signed by a church officer stating that the church you serve supports your decision to enroll in doctoral work.) Any plans that involve the help of your secretary or the ministers who work with you will need to fit within the demands that they already have to meet. Make sure that your action plan includes the consultation of those your new commitments will affect. At other times, even when it is not necessary to involve others in the pursuit of your goals, you may want to include the advice of others in your action plan.

For example, consider a minister of education who sets a personal goal to read six devotional classics within the next year. Though it would not be necessary to seek the advice of others, the minister may plan to contact several colleagues for recommendations of good devotional reading.

Question 4:

"In what sequence must I perform each action?"

The more activity required to achieve a goal, the more necessary it becomes to answer this question. The best way to prepare an action plan that involves a number of important steps is to write down the steps as they come to your mind. Pay no attention to what order the steps should take. Then, when you are certain that you have included every action necessary to reach your goal, decide the sequence the actions require. Number the activities depending on which should come first, second, third, and so on. In this way, you have a carefully prepared plan for fulfilling your commitment.

Question 5:

"When must I have each action accomplished?"

Just as your goals require deadlines, so do the activities in your plan of action. By attaching deadlines, you make sure to give yourself time to order materials, preregister for conferences, consult others, and perform the additional steps necessary to accomplish a goal.

The most important reason for stitching deadlines onto your action plan, though, is the motivating power that deadlines provide. I read about one twenty-five-year-old who discovered the value of these mini-deadlines when she set out to become a medical doctor. At first Jan McBarron was immobilized by the overwhelming distance she would have to cross to become a doctor. Then she saw that reaching medical school involved a series of steps with built-in deadlines. "Rather than dread deadlines, I used them," she says. "Applications had to be in by a certain date, assignments completed at a certain time. Once I saw what deadlines could do, I began setting my own." Now in her late thirties, Dr. McBarron enjoys a private practice in Georgia.[2]

The doctor's experience illustrates the value in using deadlines. First, deadlines on your action plan break down an intimidating goal to manageable proportions. Second, accomplishing an activity by a set deadline becomes a victory that motivates you to continue your progress. Deadlines become milestones that help you mark your progress toward the final deadline of your goal. Be sure to include deadlines in your action plan.

By the way, I have found it helpful to make a short reference to the deadlines in my pocket calendar. As I plan my schedule, the note in my calendar reminds me when the accomplishment of an action plan is due.

STORIES FROM THE FRONT LINES

Think through what methods you will use, what costs you will incur, whom you should consult or enlist, what sequence the actions should take, and when you should complete each action. Asking these five questions of your goals will help you prepare action plans for your commitments. By mapping out exactly how you plan to achieve your goals, you are more likely to reach them.

What follows are fictional accounts of the action plans certain ministers might set. The stories are intended to illustrate how we can become more effective ministers if we will review our ministries by means of written manifestos, set goals from our evaluations, and set action plans that navigate our work toward our goals. Though the accounts are fictional, perhaps you will see yourself or those you know.

The Preschool Director Who Wanted to Develop a Prayer Plan

"A clean desk is the sign of a sick mind!" declared the plaque on the office wall. It was the second thing a visitor to Sara's office would see—after the disheveled desktop. Sara joked that she wasn't unorganized, but rather "organizationally challenged," to use the politically-correct title. Time management techniques went no further than a Hallmark datebook stuffed with "to-do" lists she had compiled on various scraps of paper that happened to be at hand when she remembered an item she had to see to.

The parents and volunteer workers at First Baptist's Preschool Ministry rarely complained over her unorthodox administrative style, though. They found Sara to be keenly attentive to their needs. Publicly, she motivated everyone with her enduring enthusiasm and endearing laughter. Privately, she counseled individuals with marvelous empathy and encouragement.

As the church year was drawing to a close, the minister of education set the date for the annual all-day planning meeting for his education team—the student minister, the part-time senior adult director, and Sara. Copies of a book on personal goal-setting were passed out and the minister of education announced that part of the retreat would be spent on planning for self-improvement. Sara thumbed through the book, calling out the managerial words as she scanned them. "Objectives . . . deadlines . . . action plans . . . goal-setting worksheets—You must be doing this for my benefit, Larry," said Sara, smiling. The student minister and the part-time senior adult minister chuckled.

But Sara found that she enjoyed preparing her mission statement. There was something energizing about focusing her entire calling into a few sentences. Returning to the group, she listened as her team shared their personal manifestos. After several suggestions from Larry and several corrections of her own, she presented the following manifesto to the education team:

1. I will set a good example of what it means to follow Jesus.

2. I will make sure that every lesson that is brought to our preschoolers is faithful to the Bible and meaningful to the age group being taught.

3. I will take every opportunity, publicly and privately, to help parents build good homes for their preschool children.

4. I will be an effective administrator of the program I lead, under the supervision of the minister of education.

5. I will equip my volunteer workers to help me make the best preschool ministry possible.

6. I will be an intercessor for the preschoolers and the adults who influence them.

After she finished reading the list to the group, Larry joked, "And you thought you wouldn't like this work!" Then he addressed the entire group, "You all did great with your mission statements. Now, we each need to get alone in the church building for thirty to forty minutes. Examine your ministry up against your manifesto and ask God to show you some areas where you need improvement."

Even as Sara stood and gathered her materials to leave, she knew at least one area of her ministry she wanted to develop. She had just completed reading a book on prayer, and it had inspired her to improve her prayer life. As she settled into a comfortable chair in the unoccupied church library, she sipped on coffee and quietly committed to become more consistent in prayer for the preschoolers, parents, and volunteer workers in the ministry she led. She identified other areas for self-improvement, but intercession topped her list. She was convinced that no number of programs she planned or counseling sessions she held would be effective if she did not join her efforts with consistent intercessory prayer.

Returning to the planning meeting, Sara listened as Larry presented the criteria of well-written goals and action plans that should come from the raw material of self-evaluation. Following the presentation, Larry turned to his preschool director. "Sara," Larry began, "you can be our guinea pig! Give me an area you feel God wants you to develop and we'll turn it into a goal and make an action plan." Sara mentioned her desire to develop a more consistent intercessory prayer life.

"Okay, team," Larry said as he looked around the group, "what would be a good goal for Sara to set?" Several suggestions were offered and Larry scribbled them on a dry-erase board. Finally, Sara was pleased with the following goal: "From January 1 to May 31, I will commit the first thirty minutes of each office day to pray for those who are touched by my ministry."

At first, Sara did not want to limit her commitment to six months. But Larry convinced her that the May 31 deadline was simply a date to review her progress. He assured her that she would be more likely to stick to the habit of intercessory prayer if she set a date at which she would be able to stop and reassess her goal. If she found the goal manageable after six months, she could easily extend the deadline. After a time, Larry told her, the habit would be so much a part of her office day that she would not need to set a goal.

"Team," Larry continued, tapping the goal on the board for emphasis, "what steps will Sara have to take to make sure this commitment becomes a part of her life?" The youth minister grinned and began, "She will need to block out thirty minutes a day in that Hallmark datebook of hers." The senior-adult minister added, "And she will need to make some kind of list or file with the names of the preschoolers, the parents, and the volunteers." Sara said, "I'll need to decide how to divide that list to make it manageable." After some further discussion, the following action plan had been written on the board:

1. By the first week of November, I will submit to the printing shop a design for a prayer-gram to be used to write to those I will pray for.

2. By the first week of December, I will compile three sets of cards—one set on my preschool students and their parents, one set on prospects for enrollment, and one set on my volunteer workers. I will leave enough space on each card to write in specific prayer requests that might come to my attention.

3. By the second week of December, I will feature my prayer goal in my weekly newsletter column. I will encourage people to let me know how I can pray for them.

4. By the first full office week in January, I will begin my intercessory routine. Each Tuesday and Wednesday, I will pray for enrolled preschool students and their parents. I will pray for a few each week so that I have lifted up every enrolled family per month. Each Thursday, I will pray for my workers, especially noting the needs that were raised during Wednesday night worker's meeting. Each Friday, I will pray for the prospects—especially those I visited during the Thursday night visitation program.

5. By the last Friday in May, I will meet with Larry to review my progress on this goal.

The goal-setting continued until Larry and his staff had announced their goals and action plans. The minister of education complimented them on their efforts and then closed in prayer. "Father," he began, "thank You for speaking to us today about the areas in which we need improvement as ministers. Help us all to fulfill these goals we've set under Your guidance. When we stand before You in heaven, may we hear You say, 'Well done, good and faithful servants.' Amen." Sara thought about her goal of intercessory prayer and nodded assent to Larry's prayer. "Amen," she said to herself. "Let it be."

The Associate Pastor Who Wanted to Develop His People Skills

Wayne sat in his office with the door closed and the blinds drawn. Although his desk was usually a textbook example of efficiency, this Monday afternoon unopened mail and three call-back notices sat ignored on his desk. The computer file containing his journal was open and he had begun a brooding entry. It had been four hours since his annual review and he was still sulking. His pastor had listed off, one after the other, the shortcomings he believed Wayne had when it came to people skills.

Wayne's journal entry had begun as a bitter defense of his work at the church. But as he scrolled back through the paragraphs, he noticed that most of the successes he cited had nothing to do with teamwork or people development. Instead, he had listed projects such as the purchase and installation of a network of personal computers for the office suite, the development of a direct mail campaign that had resulted in two hundred new prospects, and the completion of a policy and procedure manual for the personnel. It dawned on him that none of the successes depended on the help of others. He had done the work by himself. For twenty minutes he sat motionless, his fingers resting on the keyboard, his eyes staring blankly at the screen saver.

"Maybe Steve is right," he thought. "Maybe I come up short when it comes to people skills." He thought back over the three years he had served at Valley Gate. He had never played golf with a church member, though he knew several who enjoyed the game as much as he did. As associate pastor, he had been assigned the oversight and development of the deacon body, but he had never met a deacon for breakfast to discuss ministry. In fact, he had never discussed the deacon ministry with anyone outside the monthly deacon's meeting. He was also responsible for welcoming new members into the church. On a few occasions, at his wife's prompting, a new church member was invited over for Sunday dinner. But he could think of few other contacts he had made with new members, aside from the obligatory form letter he signed and mailed the week after a new member joined.

He sighed and pulled out a file drawer from his desk. Thumbing through the meticulously-labeled files, he found the one marked "Goal-Setting Seminar." Last year, he had attended a summer conference at a christian conference center where the participants were led to write personal mission statements and review their ministries against their statements. The managerial terminology was familiar to him, and he had picked up on the process easily.

Upon reviewing his manifesto, though, two objectives now rose up from the page like accusing fingers: "I will help the deacons to be effective in the work of pastoral ministry," and "I will equip new church members to join in the life and ministry of this church." He had to admit that very little of what he had done during his three years at Valley Gate could fulfill those objectives. In fact, the goals he had set under these objectives in last year's retreat suddenly seemed sterile. Under the objective of assimilating new church members, for example, he had committed to "develop a four-week orientation class for new members." He recalled that, once he had designed the course—

by himself—he had enlisted a layperson to teach this orientation and had never attended the class personally.

He returned to his journal entry. "While I am proud of the work I have done at Valley Gate," he began typing, "further reflection on my three years here has led me to the conclusion that I need work on my people skills. I have allowed myself to become close with only a handful of people here. The distance I have maintained from others has hurt my ministry, particularly my ministry of welcoming new members into our fellowship."

He stared at the blinking cursor for a moment. Then he added, "I will make the following goal: I will set aside at least three Sundays a month to bring a new church member to dinner. I will begin this goal in two weeks and I will review my progress after nine months." Wayne walked to the window and opened the blinds, letting the springtime sun stream into his office. Staring out at the new buds forming on the trees in the church yard, the associate pastor thought about what he would have to do to make his goal a reality. His decision would affect his family's Sunday afternoon routine, so his first activity would be to run the idea by his wife. Rebecca enjoyed entertaining guests, and Wayne was certain she would agree to his goal. Still, he committed to speak with her before the week was out. In addition, he needed to maintain a record of the newcomers he hosted. He decided to have his secretary make a simple record of two columns. The first column would contain a list of new members, starting with those households who had come in the last six months and updated as new members joined. In the second column he would register the date he hosted the new family or individual for dinner. In addition, he determined to phone new members on Wednesday of each week to have a commitment from a new household before the weekend.

Wayne returned to his desk, entered the action plan into his journal, and wrote the deadlines into his datebook. Then he picked up the phone and dialed the pastor's office. "Steve, do you have a minute? I need to talk with you."

The Pastor Who Wanted to Give More Attention to His Marriage

"I'm sorry. You know I'll be praying for you, Andy," Richard said, and hung up the phone quietly. "How could they let something like this happen?" he thought as he leaned back in his office chair. He swiveled to the right and stared at a photograph mounted on a stand in his book cabinet. Smiling from the frame were the young and eager faces of Richard and his best friend, Andrew, standing together in front of the seminary chapel in graduation gowns, squinting in the sunlight. Beside them were their wives. "How could Andy and Caroline let it come to a divorce?"

Eighteen years earlier, Andrew and Richard met during their days as seminary students. Richard was a newlywed at the time, married to Natalie for only three months. He also served as director of the college ministry in a suburban church only twenty minutes from the seminary. Andrew dropped in on Richard at his church occasionally. Then he met a pretty senior in Richard's college ministry and began to attend more often. Within a year, he and Caroline were married.

Richard was jarred back to the present by a knock on his open office door. His associate pastor stood in the doorway. "Are you doing anything for lunch?" he asked.

Richard looked at his watch. "Yes, I'm meeting Natalie at the Pasta Garden. But thanks, Jim. We'll go together another day."

Later, as the waiter walked away with their order, Richard shared Andrew's news with Natalie. He let Natalie sit in silence for a moment. Plates of pasta were served, and they held hands for a brief blessing over the meal. Picking up his fork, Richard continued, "I feel for Andy and Caroline. But do you know what crossed my mind first after I hung up the phone? Our marriage. It may have been the first time in my life that I realized how fragile a relationship can be. I mean, life has been so good with you and the kids that I guess I've never considered it possible that our relationship could unravel."

Natalie nodded. "We could start taking each other for granted if we're not careful."

"I've been thinking," Richard began. "Maybe we should make a plan to strengthen our marriage—I mean, we could plan some things that would make sure that we don't take each other for granted. I know it doesn't sound very romantic. But the news about Andy and Caroline has really shaken me up. Besides, I think that it would be a good testimony for our church. There are several members whose marriages aren't doing very well. If they see us making deliberate plans to keep our marriage strong, it may motivate them to do the same thing."

"Do you have in mind things like regular dates and marriage retreats?" Natalie asked. Her husband nodded. She smiled, "I think it's a great idea. Let's set a goal to prepare an annual—what should we call it—oh, an annual *marriage enrichment plan* on the first of January each new year."

"I think the plan should include at least one weekend away, for just the two of us," Natalie added. "And at least one 'date' a month for just the two of us."

"And we should read one book about marriage together or register for one marriage seminar each year. We could also plan to attend a marriage enrichment seminar. Also, I'd like to announce our plan in the first newsletter of the new year. I think it would make us more accountable and it could motivate others to do the same thing."

Taking out his pocket calendar, Richard flipped to a clean notebook page and jotted their goal: "We will prepare a written annual marriage enrichment plan every New Year's Day." As they continued to talk about the goal, he listed the steps they would have to take to complete the goal. First, they would set aside an hour or two on the upcoming New Year's Day holiday to prepare the plan. Second, by the time of their meeting, they would be ready with suggestions on specific books to read, retreats to attend, and outings to enjoy. Third, the newsletter column about their marriage enrichment plan would have to be written by the first newsletter deadline of the new year. They agreed to write the column and sign it together as a public commitment.

Richard picked up the check and placed a tip on the table. As they left, he put his arm around his wife and grinned, "What do you think the kids will do for us on our fiftieth wedding anniversary?"

The Minister to Students Who Wanted to Be a Writer

John turned off the car radio and drove in silence. The only sound was the rhythmic swish of the wipers sweeping away the gentle rain pelting his windshield. As the youth minister drove the three hours back to his church field, his thoughts returned again to the writer's conference he had just attended at his old seminary.

The conference leader, Judi, began the conference by asking the group, "Why do you want to get your work published?" John had thought of this question for several years, and he responded immediately. "Because it can expand my teaching ministry and I can share with others what I've learned in preparing programs and lessons in my church's youth ministry." John was pleased with several of the programs he had designed and lesson plans he had prepared. Why should he limit the exposure of his programs and lesson plans to the high school students that attended his youth program? By becoming a writer, he could expand his teaching ministry.

But until now, writing for publication had been so intimidating that he had never attempted it. What periodicals would accept his work? What topics were editors looking for? How long should an article be? Should he develop the entire article only to risk rejection, or should he send just the basic idea in a letter to the editor? Should he even send his correspondence directly to the editor, or was it more appropriate to address it to an assistant? Could he send his proposed article to more than one periodical at a time? How long should he expect to wait for a reply? The mysteries of publishing rose up against his dreams like formidable enemy troops.

An eighteen-wheeler roared by on the left, splashing John's windshield and briefly blinding him. As the wipers cleared the water, John thought about his renewed determination to be a writer. Attending the conference removed many of his old fears and inspired him to submit some of his ideas for publication. Keeping his eyes on the slick interstate, with his right hand he fumbled around the front seat until he found his microcassette recorder. He pushed the record button and began to speak.

"After this conference, I have decided to quit dreaming about being a writer and start taking the actions necessary to get my work published. To expand the teaching ministry to which God has called me, I will set a goal of getting one article published by the end of this year." He pressed the pause button, collecting his thoughts. The wording needed to be changed. He had no control over whether an editor accepted his work. "Scratch that last line," he continued, "To expand the teaching ministry to which God has called me, I will set a goal of submitting three of my proposed articles to nine publications before this year is through."

Judi had told the participants that in most cases, instead of sending a complete unsolicited manuscript, prospective writers should send the editor a "query letter" outlining the proposed article and the author's qualifications for writing the article. If the editor is interested, the writer may be asked to send the complete article "on speculation"—that is, without obligation to publish it. Judi added that most editors do not mind query letters being sent to more than one periodical at a time. John's goal was to send one query to one set of editors, another query to another set of editors, and a third query to a third set, so that he had communicated with nine periodicals in a year's time. He turned his recorder off and laid it beside him as he thought through the year-long process he would have to take to reach his goal.

He knew that he would have to research the market to discover which publications would be most receptive to his ideas. Also, he would have to have the names of the editors and their guidelines for submissions. The names of the editors could be found in the latest issues of the periodicals. From most publishers he could request writer's guidelines and a current copy of the publication by simply sending the newsstand cost and a self-addressed stamped envelope. He decided to spend the first quarter of the next year simply researching the market for youth-oriented material. He would then spend the next three quarters submitting ideas, one query a quarter.

He turned on his recorder. "First," he began, "I will develop a markets file. I will return to my seminary library to find publications oriented toward youth ministry. I will also consult the current copy of *Writer's Market* at my local library.[3] I will request writer's guidelines and a current copy of the periodical from every editor I find. As the material is sent to me, I will file it away, dedicating a separate folder for each publication. My markets file should be completed within the first three months of the new year.

"Second," he continued, "by the end of the second quarter, I will send to three editors a query letter offering an article about using contemporary secular songs in Bible studies for students." He had enjoyed some success in his Wednesday night Bible studies by playing recordings of popular secular music and discussing the lyrics with the students. He believed that the article could be sent to publications aimed at youth workers.

"Third, by the end of the third quarter, I will send to another three editors a query letter offering an article to students about the value and the process of memorizing Scripture." His students had often expressed appreciation to him for introducing them to his process of memorizing Scripture. He believed that a publication aimed at high school students would be receptive to the piece.

"Fourth, by the end of the fourth quarter, I will send to another three editors a query letter offering an article designed to help pastors better relate to the youth pastors they have on staff." John smiled as he added into the recorder, "I'll title it, 'What Your Youth Pastor Always Wanted to Tell You.'" He had served on staff under three pastors, and he believed that he could offer some helpful advice to pastors in relating to their staffs. Perhaps his article could find its way into *Leadership* journal or *Church Administration* or another publication aimed at pastors and staff administrators.

John turned off his recorder and turned his radio back to his favorite oldies station. Tapping his fingers on the steering wheel, he began to sing along to the Beatles tune. Suddenly he stopped singing and laughed as he recognized the song—"Paperback Writer."

A ROAD MAP

An intentional minister not only prepares goals in keeping with his or her objectives but also the minister thinks through the steps that he will have to take to achieve the goals. An action plan serves as a road map, helping the minister determine the best route to take in pursuit of self-improvement. Use the following activity as an opportunity to map out your route to success.

ACTIVITY

Most likely, you have already begun to think about the steps you must take to complete the goals you wrote in chapter 4. Think about your goals in relation to the five questions that were asked in chapter 5, and then prepare an action plan for each of your goals.

Make several copies of the following page, entitled "Action Plan Worksheet." Place your first objective in the space provided and write the goal you prepared for that objective

---

Make several copies of the following page, entitled "Action Plan Worksheet." Place your first objective in the space provided and write the goal you prepared for that objective in the second box. The steps of your action plan should be entered, in sequence, in the third box. Do the same with your other goals.

ACTION PLAN WORKSHEET

Objective:

_____

_____

_____

Goal:

_____

_____

_____

Action Plan	*Deadline*

1. _____   _____

_____

_____

2. _____   _____

_____

_____

3. _____   _____

_____

_____

4. _____   _____

_____

_____

5. _____   _____

_____

_____

SIX

NOW WHAT?

You can't build a reputation on what you're going to do.

—Henry Ford

Stephen Covey calls them habits. You ought to pick up a copy of his best-seller, *The Seven Habits of Highly Effective People*. In the book, Covey outlines the patterns of behavior in successful people. The first three habits are described as "private victories"—inward habits of character that help a person move from a state of helplessness over his situation to a state of competent independence. Only as the first three habits are underway can a person ever hope to master the next three habits. These are described as "public victories"—outward expressions of character that lead a person to vital and productive interdependence with others. The seventh habit sustains the process of growth.

I suppose much of what has been presented in this book would be grouped in Covey's category of "private victories." You can gain the victory in becoming the minister Christ has called you to be when you hammer out a personal mission statement, measure yourself against it, and set manageable goals for self-improvement in the power of the Holy Spirit.

It is instructive that Covey deliberately called these behaviors *habits*. The effective minister does not file and forget his personal mission statement after writing it. The effective staff member does not refer to her self-improvement goals simply during an annual performance review. It must become habitual to justify every ministry activity by means of your manifesto. It must become customary for you to set new goals as periodic self-examinations reveal areas that need strengthening. It must become part of your weekly routine to monitor the progress you've made toward your goals.

The material in this book needs to become *habit-forming!* The American educator, Horace Mann, emphasized the importance of habits. "Habit is a cable," he said. "We weave a thread of it every day and at last we cannot break it." We ministers need to weave the practices of self-improvement into our daily routines until they become unbreakable cables. Let me make several suggestions for integrating the four steps of this book into your ministry routine.

MAKE YOUR MANIFESTO
A POINT OF REFERENCE

It was a fog-shrouded morning, July 4, 1952, when Florence Chadwick tried to swim the channel between Catalina Island and the coast of California. Long-distance swimming was nothing new to her; Chadwick had been the first woman to swim the English Channel in both directions.

Stepping into the numbing cold water, however, she could hardly see the boats in her party for the fog. Fifteen hours later, she asked to be taken out of the water. Her trainer tried to encourage her—she only had a short distance left. But wherever Chadwick looked, all she saw was fog. So she quit—one-half mile from her goal.

She said of the experience later, "I'm not excusing myself, but if I could have seen the land I might have made it." She did not fail because of the cold water, the exhaustion, or the fear of sharks that her party had to drive away with rifle fire. It was the inability to see her destination. Two months later, Chadwick walked off the same beach into the same channel and swam the distance—even setting a new speed record—because she could see the land. She needed to locate her mark in order to be successful. For the same reason, we need to make our objectives and goals a point of reference. The following are ways to "burn off the fog" and keep our mark ever before us.

Create and Display a Model of Your Objectives

Having a pictoral diagram of your objectives will help you remember the priorities of your calling. In fact, it was a picture of three interlocking circles that gave many of us our first comprehensive picture of the demands of ministry (see fig. 6.1).

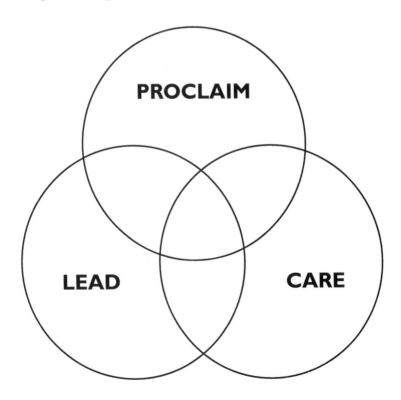

Figure 6.1: Mosley Ministry Model I

Ernest Mosley first introduced this construct in his book, *Called to Joy*. The church leader must *lead* the church in the achievement of its mission, *proclaim* the gospel, and *care* for the church's members and other persons in the community. The three interlocking circles have been a visual reminder to countless ministers that they must not regard one task as more important than another task, and they must not perform one responsibility independently of the other two.

It is difficult to improve on such a balanced presentation of the responsibilities of the pastor and his associates on staff. But I have tried! I have my own visual construct: four arrows proceeding from a central circle. (see fig. 6.2).

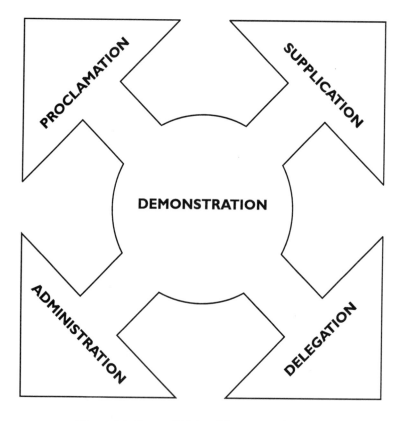

Figure 6.2: Responsibilities of Pastor and Associates

The visual model helps me remember that the most important task of the ministry is developing a demonstrable fellowship with Jesus. Out of that springs the other tasks. The arrows remind me that I should always be in the process of developing myself.

I would not be surprised if, by this point in the book, you already have some way to visualize your objectives. I remember the first time I led a seminar on becoming an intentional minister. In one of the exercises, the church leaders were given forty minutes to write their own manifestos (as you were asked to do at the end of chap. 2). Each minister was given time at a large dry-erase board to present his manifesto.

I imagined that the church leaders would simply list their objectives in some numerical order. Instead, nearly all of them had prepared a diagram of their objectives. One visualized his manifesto in the form of a pyramid, with what he regarded as the foundational objective forming the base. A second used building blocks, which helped him remember that his ministry was "under construction." Another drew concentric circles, labeling the inner rings with his most important priorities. Another used a wagon wheel, labeling a spoke with each objective. The image reminded him of the importance of his "hub" objective and the need to make sure all the "spokes" were working to ensure the entire wheel did not collapse. One outlined his objectives in the shape of a cross.

In fact, one of the participants who was skilled with crafts announced he was planning to design a woodworking of his manifesto. He wanted his standard of success prominently displayed on his office wall as a visual reminder of what Christ had called him to be. Why not stop a moment and doodle a few diagrams on some blank paper until you have your own pictoral diagram of ministry?

Include Your Objectives and the Pursuit of Your Goals as You Make Journal Entries

If you have a personal journal, insert your goal sheets at the front. As you fulfill the action plans, record the date on the goal sheet. Use your journal entries to reflect on your progress.

Gordon MacDonald makes it a routine to review his life against the personal mission statement inserted in his journal. MacDonald has written several books on personal development such as *Ordering Your Private World* and *Renewing Your Spiritual Passion*. He has inserted his manifesto in the front of his journal and he turns to it every morning to start his day. He says it "defines my direction and channels my enthusiasm."[1]

Use Your Manifesto and Goals When Planning Your Weekly Schedule

This will enable you to see the amount of time you are devoting to your various objectives. For example, a youth director may have an objective of developing volunteer leaders for the work of youth ministry. As he examines his calendar in light of his objective, however, he finds that two months have gone by without a personal contact with any of his volunteer leaders. The next week, he schedules visits with three workers.

Stephen Covey has created a weekly worksheet for this purpose. One can enter objectives and weekly goals in a left-hand column and then enter the actual time one plans to spend on those goals in a daily appointment calendar. Covey described his worksheets in *The Seven Habits* and in a free *Personal Leadership Application Workbook* available from the Covey Leadership Center.

The point is, you should refer frequently to your manifesto and to your goals. Like Florence Chadwick off the coast of California, we can give up in exhaustion and frustration if we cannot locate the end result of our labors. To teach their principles of management, Kenneth Blanchard and Spencer Johnson created the mythical one-minute manager. This manager had a plaque displayed at each work-station with the following four lines. Maybe a plaque like this on our desks would help us become more effective:

Take a Minute:
Look at Your Goals.
Look at Your Performance.
See If Your Behavior Matches Your Goals.2

Keeping your concept of effective ministry before you is not a new technique. Richard Baxter recommended it over three hundred years ago in *The Reformed Pastor.* He wrote:

> Keep up earnest desires and expectations of success. If your heart be not set on the end of your labors, and you long not to see the conversion and edification of your hearers, and do not study and preach in hope, you are not likely to see much fruit of it. . . . So I have observed that God seldom blesses any man's work so much as his whose heart is set upon success.[3]

EDUCATE THE LAITY

"I hope this doesn't sound insulting," began a friend of mine, "but what do you *do* all day?" I laughed and used the opportunity to share my priorities and my weekly schedule with him. Even the most supportive church members are often unaware of what our jobs involve. After we have mapped out our priorities, we should use every opportunity to share them with the laity.

Within Your Own Congregation

Lead your congregation to understand your role. A pastor could take a Sunday evening service to present his manifesto to his church, making each objective a point in the sermon. If you serve in a staff position, perhaps your pastor would give you a Sunday night or mid-week service to share your priorities with the congregation. Or why not use your column in the church newsletter to highlight your convictions and announce your personal goals? The pastor who leads a staff might ask each staff member to share his or her mission statement during a staff appreciation dinner. At the very least, a staff member needs to share his convictions with the layleaders of the program he leads.

Upon Considering a Move

An ideal time to lead churches to understand your role is at the start of service in a new field. In *A Glad Beginning—A Gracious Ending*, D. L. Lowrie suggests that when a pastor is considering a new church, he should present his manifesto—what Lowrie calls a "role description"—at the first meetings with the leadership. In this way he can avoid some of the misunderstandings that arise when minister and church mistakenly assume that each shares the priorities of the other.[4] Of course, this has application to all staff, not just the pastor.

In Times of Tension

Another time to communicate your convictions is when a deep misunderstanding of your role develops between you and your church. In his book, *Forced Termination*, Brooks Faulkner urges that an attempt at retraining should always come before forced termination. Faulkner suggests that the minister and church leadership organize a retreat at which together they can come to an agreement on the minister's priorities.[5]

MAKE TIME FOR EVALUATION

In chapter 3, I suggested that the intentional minister performs checkups for personal and professional improvement. He examines his ministry himself, and he enlists the help of others to review the performance of his objectives. In order for this to become habitual, you will want to be aware of the human and material resources available for performance reviews.

Resources for Self-Evaluations

Plan to purchase a *Personal Profile System* soon. The profile helps a person discover his behavioral patterns as he relates to others. The *Personal Profile System* can be purchased through a number of outlets, such as the Leadership Training Division of Walk Thru the Bible Ministries. WTB has incorporated the profile into a series of leadership training modules that can help you not only interpret the results of your own profile, but also administer the evaluation to others.

Resources for Surveying Your Congregation

In chapter 3, I suggested some ways to elicit feedback from those you serve. For more guidance in creating survey forms for use in performance reviews, see Lee Kageler's "Performance Reviews: Worth the Trouble?" and Knute Larson's "How I Rate Me." Both of these articles were published in the Summer 1985 issue of *Leadership*. The same journal also published "Performance Reviews: Avoiding the Pitfalls," by Larry Osborne in the Summer 1988 issue.

To make it easier to process the data you receive from large surveys, consider using computer software programs like *Gaining Insights*.[6] It is a tool for performing market research that has been adapted for churches. It helps you assess the needs, attitudes, and feelings of the congregation and break down those opinions by respondents' variables (such as age, length of membership, education, and so on). Once the data is entered, the statistical analysis is tallied quickly and the results are presented by means of charts, graphs (bar, pie, line, stacked bar), and summary reviews. The program was originally designed to gather opinions on the ministries of the church, but the survey questions can be tailored to gather opinions on the ministers of the church, too.

Resources for Professional Evaluation

In addition to the important assessment from those we serve, another source for feedback is a career-assessment consultation. Most denominations have resources and seminars that provide professional guidance for reflecting on ministry issues. Contact your headquarters for help.

TAKE AN ANNUAL RETREAT FOR REFLECTION AND PLANNING

We read in the Gospels that Jesus often withdrew from those He served to be alone with His Father. If Jesus found a need for this kind of isolation, how much more do we need it! Such isolated time for reflection and renewal is needed in brief, regular doses throughout the year. Make sure to give yourself and your staff prolonged retreats. Those who claim that they do not have the time for such reflection and planning remind me of the fabled lumberjack who felt he could not take the time to sharpen his ax. Eventually he was investing more and more energy and finding fewer and fewer results.

Personal Planning

Use your manifesto to evaluate your ministry and to set new goals for further improvement. I read of one pastor and his wife who spend New Year's Day evaluating the past year. Together they set goals for church life, financial commitments, family enrichment, and areas of personal development. I prefer to take a couple of days in late July or early August, before the new church calendar begins in October. I take my planning materials and get away from the church field for evaluation and planning.

Leading Staff to Plan for Self-Improvement

Some churches have annual planning retreats to review and improve the church programs. Again, make sure that your annual planning to improve the church's ministries includes time for planning to improve the church's ministers. The time given to staff for self-renewal is not a luxury; it has a direct impact on the quality of church programs. In fact, the success of a program goal may *depend* on whether a staff member sets a personal goal to improve a personal leadership quality. Before your next staff planning retreat, why not order enough copies of *The Intentional Minister* for your team? You could give them time to work through the activities during your retreat.

ASK OTHERS TO HELP YOU FULFILL YOUR GOALS

Counselor Alan McGinnis complains that many of his clients try various techniques for self-improvement while overlooking the best source for help—good friendships.[7] Involve others in the pursuit of your goals. By welcoming the help of others, you will gain new ideas for pursuing your goals and you will find the accountability needed to succeed in your goals.

Gain New Ideas for Pursuing Your Goals

You could take some time to ask other ministers what they are doing to improve in the areas in which you want to improve. The resulting conversation will always be more interesting than idly chatting about last Sunday's attendance. For example, consider a youth minister who wants to become more of an encourager to his students and to those who influence them. He could offer to buy lunch for a more experienced youth minister who is known for his ability to be a positive motivator. The more experienced youth minister could be asked to provide suggestions for forming and reaching a goal in this area.

I remember the help I received from several ministers when a church I once served set a baptism goal. We planned to baptize 6 percent of our Sunday School enrollment number annually. I researched the records in the local Baptist association to find at least ten churches in our area that regularly met or exceeded that baptism ratio. I called the pastors and held an informal telephone interview with them. Most of the ministers were surprised and complimented by the phone call. I received affirmation regarding efforts we had already begun, and I was given suggestions regarding efforts they felt I should start. Some lasting friendships have developed from those phone calls. And, after years of baptizing less than 1 percent of our Sunday School enrollment number annually, our church exceeded our new goal every year I served there.

Find the Accountability Needed to Succeed in Your Goal

The intentional minister welcomes not only the suggestions that others provide for pursuing his self-improvement plan, but also the accountability that others provide for sticking to his self-improvement plan. The following are suggestions, in descending order of value, for making yourself accountable to another.

First, the most helpful plan of accountability would be to gather two or three ministers from other churches who serve in the same position as you do and begin a minister's support group. A support group of our peers has the wider purpose of providing ethical accountability and emotional assistance. In addition though, the group can be a place to receive the advice, accountability, and prayer support that we need in the pursuit of our goals. A helpful resource for beginning a support group is *Minister's Support Group: Alternative to Burnout*, by Charles Chandler.

Second, if you don't have a support group, make yourself accountable by telling someone you trust about the goals you intend to achieve. Tell a marriage partner, a deacon, or a fellow staff member. Knowing that someone is praying for you and that periodically he or she will ask you about your progress will be a strong motivator to fulfill your goals.

Third, take advantage of the accountability structure built into your church's organization. If your church does annual performance reviews, provide a written copy of your goals to your reviewers before the evaluation. Ask them to include questions about your goals in next year's performance review. In churches that do not hold formal performance reviews, a pastor could share his goals with the deacon body and staff members could share their goals with the volunteer workers in the programs they lead. In turn, ministers could challenge the reviewers to set personal goals for their own work.

At the very least, announce your goals in the church newsletter, ask for prayer, and publish your progress from time to time. Accountability is vital to the success of your self-improvement plan. I cannot always trust myself to evaluate my progress. According to the Word of God, "The heart is deceitful above all things and beyond cure."[8] I need others to help me "hold my feet to the fire."

CELEBRATE YOUR VICTORIES

As you fulfill a goal, or even as you complete some important step in your action plan, stop to savor your progress and give thanks to God. Celebrate your progress with those to whom you have made yourself accountable. Make a note of the victory in your journal. Treat yourself to something special. By recognizing these victories, you are acknowledging the activity of God in your life, and you are building your confidence for further self-improvement.

In 1 Samuel 7, we are told of an uprising of the Philistines that sent fear into all of Israel. "Do not stop crying out to the Lord our God for us," the people pleaded, "that he may rescue us from the hand of the Philistines" (v. 8). The priest sacrificed to the Lord and prayed, and God answered. The Philistines were thrown into a panic when the Lord "thundered with loud thunder" (v. 10). As a result, Israel easily routed their opponents. In commemoration of the Lord's help, Samuel set up a stone and called it Ebenezer, which means "stone of help." He explained the marker to the people, saying, "Thus far has the Lord helped us" (v. 12). That is the reference behind Robert Robinson's second stanza in his mid-eighteenth century hymn, "Come, Thou Fount of Every Blessing": "Here I raise mine Ebenezer; Hither by thy help I'm come."[9]

I confess that I need to be more consistent in "raising Ebenezers" at points of victory in my personal ministry and in the programs I lead. Too often I complete a personal goal, or the congregation reaches a church-wide goal, and I rush ahead to tackle the next one. As a result, I fail to let myself or my people celebrate and acknowledge how God has helped us. If you are like me, we should write, "Throw a party," as the last item on the action plans for our goals. In the written plans for a goal, we should set a date to stop and savor the completion of that goal.

COMMIT TO ONGOING DEVELOPMENT

We are innundated with mail promoting the latest book, workshop, or periodical. We need to make intelligent decisions regarding where to spend our limited time and money. The mail-out promoting that evangelism conference at that megachurch looks appealing. But will the conference address the areas needing improvement that you have identified? And what about that new book with the glossy cover on using drama in worship services? The idea may be trendy, but will the money and time you invest in the book actually help you toward the goals you have already set? Intentional ministers are purposeful in the books they buy, the seminars they attend, and the articles they read.

Choosing Workshops and Seminars

Choosing training opportunities will be made more intelligently now that you have defined your priorities and identified the areas in which you want to grow. Consider workshops and seminars that address your priorities. Or you may want to enroll in a Doctor of Ministry program with your professional growth in mind.

Developing Your Personal Library

Take an inventory of your library. Do your reading materials reflect a desire to develop in *all* areas of your calling? Perhaps you have an abundance of Bible study aids but very few books on counseling. Again, a review of your library may turn up numerous books on administration but very few on spiritual growth. Decide to develop your library so that you are reading materials on all aspects of your ministry.

Forming a Vertical File

Do you have a way of saving unbound material that addresses your ministry objectives? Create space in your filing cabinet for gathering magazine articles and handouts from seminars. Label each file folder with a separate objective. Then, as you receive an inspirational handout from a conference or as you run across a helpful article in a periodical, file it in the appropriate folder for future reference.

A TIME FOR ACTION

The point is, being a minister on purpose needs to be habit-forming. Your manifesto will need some periodic fine-tuning. You will have to get into practice saying no to activities that do not move you toward your objectives. You will need to set new goals as reviews of your ministry turn up areas to develop. You will need to include "pit stops" in your busy schedule at which you stop and celebrate the progress you have been making in your self-improvement plan. These are some habits that make highly effective ministers.

Our planning is over and the time for action is here. We are at a dangerous time in our efforts at self-improvement! At this point we can fail to follow through on all of our elaborate planning. Business tycoon T. Boone Pickens said it best. While speaking at a college commencement, he told the students, "Don't fall victim to what I call the ready-aim-aim-aim-aim syndrome. You must be willing to fire."[10] Now that you have planned your work, work your plan!

ACTIVITY

Accountability will make or break the success of any self-improvement plan. Make yourself accountable to fulfill the goals you have made while reading this book! Choose one activity from the following list:

☐ Provide written copies of your goals to your support group or prayer partners and ask them to check your progress periodically.

☐ If your church does annual performance reviews, provide a written copy of your goals for your reviewers. Ask them to include questions about your goals in next year's performance review.

☐ If you are a pastor, share your goals with the deacon body. If you hold a staff position, share your goals with the volunteer leaders of the program you lead. In turn, challenge them to set personal goals for their own work.

☐ Announce your goals in the church newsletter and publish your progress from time to time.

☐ Write your own method of accountability:

_____

_____

_____

_____

_____

_____

_____

_____

_____

_____

NOTES

Introduction

1. Craig Brian Larson, "The Pastor as Survivalist," *Leadership*, Winter 1990, 93.

2. Phil. 3:13b–14.

3. John Haggai, *Lead On!* (Waco: Word, 1986), 18.

4. 1 Cor. 4:7.

Chapter 1: Where There Is No Vision, the Minister Perishes!

1. Matt. 25:21, 23.

2. Prov. 29:18, KJV.

3. Jer. 9:2.

4. Charles Hummel, *Tyranny of the Urgent* (Downers Grove: Intervarsity, 1967), 15.

5. R. Alec MacKenzie, *New Time Management Methods for You and Your Staff* (Chicago: Dartnell Company, 1975), 75.

6. See Matt. 25:14–30; 1 Cor. 4:1–2; 9:16–17; Col. 1:24–26; 1 Pet. 4:10.

7. Ari Kiev, *A Strategy for Daily Living* (New York: Free Press, 1973), 30, quoted in Haggai, John, *Lead On!*, 38.

8. George E. Sweazey, "The Place of Ambition in the Ministry," *The Princeton Seminary Bulletin* 60, February 1967, 39.

9. Peter Drucker, "An Interview with Peter Drucker," *The Christian Ministry*, September 1972, 8.

10. Doug Sherman and William Hendricks, *Your Work Matters to God* (Colorado Springs: Navpress, 1987), 35.

11. 1 Tim. 3:1.

12. John Henry Jowett, *The Preacher: His Life and Work* (New York: Harper and Brothers, 1912), 23–24, *Jowett's emphasis.*

13. Donald P. Smith, *Clergy in the Crossfire: Coping with Role Conflicts in the Ministry* (Philadelphia: Westminster, 1973), 86.

14. Charles Paul Conn, *Making It Happen: A Christian Looks at Money, Competition, and Success* (Old Tappan, N.J.: F.H. Revell Co., 1981), 95.

15. John W. Alexander, *Managing Our Work*, 2d rev. ed. (Downer's Grove: Intervarsity Press, 1975), 33–34.

16. Kent and Barbara Hughes, *Liberating Ministry from the Success Syndrome* (Wheaton: Tyndale, 1987), 21–22.

17. In Merrill E. and Donna N. Douglass, *Manage Your Time, Manage Your Work, Manage Yourself* (New York: AMACOM, 1980), 79.

18. Ernest Mosley, *Priorities in Ministry* (Nashville: Convention Press, 1978), 10.

19. Sharon Massey, "But to Enter, You Have to Find Stamps and Envelopes and Stuff," *The Wall Street Journal*, 2 June 1993, B1.

Chapter 2: The First Step: Create Your "Ministry Manifesto"

1. In Winston Crawley, *Global Mission* (Nashville: Broadman, 1985), 183.

2. Deut. 17:18–20.

3. David S. Schuller, Milo L. Brekke, and Merton Strommen, *Readiness for Ministry*, (Vandalia, Ohio: Association of Theological Schools, 1975), Volume I, *Criteria*. David S. Schuller, Milo L. Brekke, Merton Strommen, and Daniel Aleshire, *Readiness for Ministry*, Volume II, *Assessment* (Vandalia, Ohio: Association of Theological Schools, 1976). For a review of the "status quo" procedure, see James E. Dittes,

"Tracking God's Call: Basic Theoretical Issues in Clergy Assessment," in *Clergy Assessment and Career Development*, eds. Richard A. Hunt, John E. Hinkle, and H. Newton Malony (Nashville: Abingdon, 1990), 25.

4. 2 Tim. 4:3.

5. Ernest E. Mosley, *Called to Joy: A Design for Pastoral Ministries* (Nashville: Convention Press, 1973), 24–25.

6. Mosley, *Priorities in Ministry*, 12–13.

7. C. W. Brister, James L. Cooper, and J. David Fite, *Beginning Your Ministry*, (Nashville: Abingdon, 1981), 89.

8. John B. Aker, "Juggling: The Ministerial Art," *Leadership* 7, no. 3 (1986): 26–31.

9. Hughes, *Liberating Ministry*,

10. Richard Baxter, quoted in "The Oversight of Ourselves," *Tabletalk*, June 1992, 18.

11. 1 Tim. 4:16; see also 3:2–7; 4:7; 6:11; 2 Tim. 1:14; 2:24–26; 4:5; Titus 1:6–9.

12. 1 Cor. 9:27; see also Jas. 3:1.

13. 1 Tim. 4:11; see also Titus 2:7.

14. 1 Pet. 5:3.

15. Phil. 3:17; see also 4:9; Heb. 13:7.

16. Acts 6:2–4.

17. 1 Tim. 3:2; see also 2 Tim. 2:24–26; Titus 2:15.

18. Titus 2:7–8.

19. 2 Tim. 4:1–2; see also 1 Tim. 4:13; 2 Tim. 2:15.

20. Floyd Doud Shafer, *Christianity Today*, 27 March 1962.

21. Acts 20:20.

22. John Calvin, *The Acts of the Apostles 14–28*, vol. 7, *Calvin's Commentaries*, trans. John W. Fraser (Grand Rapids: Eerdmans, reprinted 1973), 175.

23. 2 Tim. 4:2.

24. Jowett, *The Preacher*, 177.

25. 1 Pet. 2:9.

26. Col. 3:16.

27. Titus 1:9.

28. 2 Tim. 2:15.

29. J. M. Houston, "Spirituality," in *Evangelical Dictionary of Theology*, ed. Walter A. Elwell (Grand Rapids: Baker, 1984), 1050.

30. 1 Cor. 12:28.

31. Rom. 12:8.

32. 1 Tim. 5:17; 1 Tim. 3:5; 1 Thess. 5:12.

33. Charles A. Tidwell, *Church Administration* (Nashville: Broadman, 1985), 34.

34. 2 Tim. 2:2.

35. Eph. 4:12.

36. 1 Pet. 2:9 and 4:10.

37. Acts 6:4.

38. Jas. 5:14.

39. Curtis Vaughan, *James* (Grand Rapids: Zondervan, 1969), 117.

40. Col. 4:12.

41. Col. 1:7.

42. Richard Foster, *Money, Sex and Power: The Challenge of the Disciplined Life* (San Francisco: Harper and Row, 1985), 235–36.

43. Darius Salter, *What Really Matters in Ministry: Profiling Pastoral Success in Flourishing Churches* (Grand Rapids: Baker, 1990), 159.

44. Heb. 13:17.

45. 1 Thess. 2:19.

46. Phil. 2:14–16.

47. 2 Cor. 3:2–3.

48. F. F. Bruce, *Paul: Apostle of the Heart Set Free* (Grand Rapids: Eerdmans, 1977), 459.

Chapter 3: The Second Step: A Personal Checkup

1. Anastasia Toufexis, "Engineering the Perfect Athlete," *Time*, 3 August 1992, 58–63.

2. Brister, Cooper, and Fite, *Beginning Your Ministry*, 122.

3. Prov. 16:3.

4. Jas. 4:13–15.

5. Larry Lewis, "Inside MissionsUSA," *Missions USA*, January–February 1989, 1.

6. Matt. 16:21–23.

7. Salter, *What Really Matters in Ministry*, 168.

8. 1 Pet. 5:4.

9. Alan Loy McGinnis, "How to Get the Most Out of Yourself," *Reader's Digest*, March 1988, 196.

10. 1 Cor. 3:11–15.

11. Matt. 25:14–30.

12. Kennon Callahan, *Twelve Keys to an Effective Church* (San Francisco: Harper and Row, 1983), xvi–xvii.

13. James Gunn, "Goal-Setting and Evaluation," in *Creating an Intentional Ministry*, ed. John Biersdorf (Nashville: Abingdon, 1976), 131.

14. Fred McGehee, telephone interview by author, 13 January 1992.

15. Prov. 29:1, RSV.

16. Larry W. Osborne, "Performance Reviews: Avoiding the Pitfalls," *Leadership*, Summer 1988, 62.

17. 1 Cor. 12:18.

18. In Richard Nelson Bolles, *How to Find Your Mission in Life* (Berkeley, Calif.: Ten Speed Press, 1991), 48.

Chapter 4: The Third Step: Set Goals for Personal Improvement

1. Tom McConalogue, "Making an Effective Manager," *Management Decision* 26, May 1988: 32.

2. Edward R. Dayton, "The Urgency of Setting Goals," *The Christian Herald*, July–August 1980, 29–31.

3. Robert Jeffress, *Choose Your Attitudes, Change Your Life* (Wheaton: Victor, 1992), 133–34.

4. James Gaines, "Being Intentional with Your Ministry," *Church Administration*, November 1990, 31–32.

5. In Charles Colson, *The God of Stones and Spiders* (Wheaton: Crossway, 1990), 198.

6. George E. Sweazey, "The Place of Ambition in the Ministry," *The Princeton Seminary Bulletin* 60, February 1967: 37–40.

7. Russell Chandler, *Racing Toward 2001* (Grand Rapids: Zondervan, 1992), 217.

8. Haggai, *Lead On!*, 38.

9. Fred Smith, *Learning to Lead* (Carol Stream, Ill.: Christianity Today, Inc., 1986), 34.

10. Robert McGarvey, "Get What You Want Out of Life," *Reader's Digest*, June 1992, 106.

11. Lyle Schaller, *Survival Tactics in the Parish* (Nashville: Abingdon, 1977), 158.

12. Henry Blackaby and Claude King designed *Experiencing God: Knowing and Doing the Will of God*. It is a thirteen-week course designed to help you love God more deeply and discover His will for your life. The course has helped hundreds of thousands of people learn to find out where God is working and join Him in it. For more information, call 1-800-251-3225.

13. Robert F. Mager, *Goal Analysis* (Belmont, Calif.: Fearon Publishers, 1972), 29.

Chapter 5: The Fourth Step: Set Action Plans

1. Laurence Hooper and Jacob M. Schlesinger, "Precise Navigation Points to New Worlds," *The Wall Street Journal,* 4 March 1991, B1.

2. McGarvey, "Get What You Want," 107.

3. The *Writer's Market* is an annual publication listing the markets for publishable material. John should look at the Consumer section of the book for publications oriented to high school students, and he should look at the Trade section of the book for material aimed at youth workers. Beside the name of the publication, the *Writer's Market* lists the address, phone number, editor, and a brief description of what the editor wants from writers. The procedure for obtaining writer's guidelines and a current copy of the publication is also provided.

Chapter 6: Now What?

1. Gordon MacDonald, "What I Want to Be When I Grow Up," *Leadership,* Fall 1992, 72.

2. Kenneth Blanchard and Spencer Johnson, *The One-Minute Manager* (New York: William Morrow and Company, Inc., 1982), 74.

3. Salter, *What Really Matters in Ministry,* 101.

4. D. L. Lowrie, *A Glad Beginning—A Gracious Ending* (Nashville: Broadman, 1988), 44–46.

5. Brooks R. Faulkner, *Forced Termination* (Nashville: Broadman, 1986), 46–55.

6. Available from Church Public Relations, 26371 Bryan, Roseville, MI 48066, or call 313-771-6321.

7. McGinnis, "How to Get the Most Out of Yourself," 197.

8. Jer. 17:9.

9. In *Baptist Hymnal* (Nashville: Convention, 1975), Hymn #13.

10. "Commencement '88," *Time,* 13 June 1988, 74.